THE
GREATEST
WEEK IN HISTORY

Luke's Account of the Passion Week

LifeWay Press®
Nashville, TN

ISBN: 978-1-4158-6975-8
Item: 005367720

Subject Area: Bible Studies
Dewey Decimal Classification Number: 232.96
Subject Heading: JESUS CHRIST—PASSION WEEK \ BIBLE. N.T. LUKE—STUDY
Printed in the United States of America

Leadership and Adult Publishing
LifeWay Church Resources
One LifeWay Plaza
Nashville, TN 37234-0175

We believe the Bible has God for its author; salvation for its end; and truth, without any mixture of error, for its matter and that all Scripture is totally true and trustworthy. The 2000 statement of The Baptist Faith and Message is our doctrinal guideline.

Cover Image: IStock Photo
Chapter Beginnings: Jupiter Images Corporation
Lesson Photos: *Biblical Illustrator* Photos

Contents

The Greatest Week in History

A few years ago I had the opportunity to spend a week in Colorado on our summer vacation. My wife and I have three kids: two boys and a girl. At the time my boys were ten and seven, and my daughter was five years old. Our family lives in Madison, Mississippi, the home of great food, friendly people, and hot, humid summer days. We love our home and feel blessed to serve in what has to be one of the greatest churches in the world. But it gets really hot in the summer. Our trip came in the middle of a particularly sweltering July. It was amazing to discover that there are places in the world where people actually enjoy a full day outside in July rather than enduring a full day outside. We had a great time. We hiked miles of beautiful trails, rode mountain bikes, rafted clear rivers, fly fished in beautiful streams, went on an old-fashioned cattle round up (on horseback I might add), and ended the week with an outside barbecue at a beautiful ranch. It was an awesome week of memory-making, though I felt like I was dead broke. But just like the credit card companies promise, there was that one priceless moment. As the sun was setting, displaying God's gorgeous handiwork, I was sitting beside a blazing campfire. My daughter was sitting in my lap and the smell of barbecue was in the air. Then the payoff came! With her blue eyes sparkling, my daughter, Rivers, looked up and said, "Daddy, this was the bestest week ever!" I had to agree.

Have you ever had one of those "bestest" moments in your life? How did those times mark and bless your life? What about the "bestest" week? Do you remember seven consecutive days that touched your life and raised your expectations of what life could and should be? I hope your search down memory lane brings a smile to your face and hope to your heart. These are the significant moments that shape us. While these memories that make our favorites list are significant to us, they pale in comparison to the greatest week in history.

If someone were to ask you what was the greatest week in history, how would you answer? Many significant events have marked time. As an American, you might think about the history of the United States and the marker moments and days that shaped our country. The signing of the Declaration of Independence, Pearl Harbor, the first step on the moon, and September 11, 2001, are all etched into the minds of Americans. These dates don't just represent days; they are moments that made our nation. As significant as these dates may be within the context of modern history, they are secondary compared to the time represented in the study at hand.

Greatest Day of Your Life

Think back over your life and identify one of the greatest days you have ever experienced. It might be your wedding day, the day you received a special award, a vacation, or the day you accepted Christ. Answer the following questions:

1. What was your greatest day?

2. Can you describe some of the events leading up to that day?

3. Who was a part of the events leading up to that day?

4. Who was present on the special day?

5. Did you face any challenges leading up to that day?

Without question the greatest, most significant week in history had to be the seven days leading to and encompassing the crucifixion and resurrection of Jesus Christ. That week represents the central moment of time and eternity. No other week has impacted the world the way that one week did. Over the course of seven days, through a series of climatic events, the purpose of Jesus' ministry and mission were made clear. This, the greatest week in history, is the focus of our study.

During this study you and I will have the opportunity to observe powerful and poignant moments that made and make history. Unlike my experience as a father, our heavenly Father displayed the ultimate love through the heart-wrenching gift of His Son. This great sacrifice has become the source of all of life's greatest blessings.

A Quick Word of Introduction

Since we will be travel companions in this study, let me take a moment to introduce myself. My name is Rob Futral, and I have the unique opportunity to walk with you through those seven days that shaped the world. More able guides have studied longer, have experienced the Savior more deeply, and communicate more clearly, but I will give my very best to make our experience together memorable and beneficial. Fortunately, the way we are walking is clearly marked by some of the greatest of saints and was blazed by our great Savior. We can't go wrong if we simply stay on the trail.

You already know a little about my family from the opening story. Before we get started, I would like to tell you a few more details about myself for context. I am the son and grandson of Southern Baptist pastors (and their amazing wives). I was saved at age 12, sensed and surrendered to a call to ministry at age 15, and I have served as a pastor from age 18 to now (which is north of 40). When I surrendered to ministry, wise counsel shared that a call to ministry is a commitment to continued preparation. I have been blessed to study under many great students and teachers of God's Word in both college and seminary. Currently, I count it a privilege to be able to preach and lead weekly at Broadmoor Baptist Church in Madison, Mississippi, and to attempt to live out the gospel among a gracious community of believers. I have been blessed to travel to many parts of the world where I have seen countless unique expressions of God's church thriving. My life has been enriched and challenged to see believers across the world who love Jesus and are committed to His Great Commission. My hope is that this study will in some small way bless God's church the way His church has blessed my life.

Our Study, Our Journey

In the 66-year history of LifeWay's January Bible Study, this is the first study that focuses completely on the Passion Week. More importantly, the significant moments that shaped history have the potential to shape our lives today. For that reason I prefer to approach our subject as more than a study. Instead let's approach this as a journey that has the potential to change our lives as Jesus leads us to and through the cross.

Our Guide and Source—Luke and Luke's Passion Narrative (Luke 19:28–24:53)

Our primary resource will be the precise record found in Luke. As a physician turned partner in the gospel, Luke wrote with Gentiles in mind and desired to communicate Christ's love and message of good news to these brothers and sisters.

In his narrative, we see glimpses of Luke's unique personality and perspective, though his primary purpose in writing was not to reveal himself, but to celebrate His Savior. Luke's account of the Passion Week—the events from Palm Sunday to Resurrection Sunday—allows us to not simply read a narrative, but to walk a journey of discovery. At times we will rely on the other Gospel writers to fill in the blanks of our understanding, or perhaps round out Luke's singular perspective. Yet, for the most part we will be in the able hands of a follower of Christ who had a great desire for us to see and hear the message of the Savior of the world.

Each of the Gospel writers, led by the Holy Spirit, took great pains to share the precise nature of these moments in history. The Passion Narratives represent roughly a fourth of what the Gospel writers present to us as of utmost importance. We could infer this simply by the shear length and expanded detail of their holy record, but it is in the content of what is shared that we realize that these sections of Scripture are to be uniquely treasured.

Luke's Gospel is no different. The one week on which we are focused can be found in Luke 19:28–24:53. In addition, Luke 9:51–19:27, often called the travel narrative, has the journey to the cross as a primary theme. Other key verses, like Luke 9:23, show the centrality of the cross in the faith and practice of followers of Jesus Christ. The cross and the empty tomb are the backdrop for understanding the story that is unfolding in the narrative.

Our Approach

While a verse-by-verse study will not be possible, the major events and themes found in Luke will shape our study. Unlike most journeys, ours begins with an awareness of how the story ends. I have a habit of reading the last chapter of a book before I reach the end. I like to know how the story is going to end and I am often not patient enough to wade through the details of the story. You may be that way too. The only problem with this mind-set is that we might miss some significant moments because we are too focused on how the story ends. I challenge you to read the Bible passages as well as this study guide. Before we begin, here are a few ideas that will help us get the most out of our experience.

First of all, as we follow Jesus on this journey we should *recognize the unique viewpoints.* There is Luke's viewpoint as the author. There is the viewpoint of Jesus captured by Luke's dictation and presentation of the events and teachings. There are the viewpoints of the disciples, the crowds, religious leaders, and various others that make their way into the story line. Then, there is our viewpoint some 2,000 years later. As we follow Jesus on this journey to the cross, we will walk with Him and others as they looked forward to the cross. At the same time, we have the unique viewpoint of looking back at those events through the cross.

Second, we should *recognize that God's Word is an historical record with a present implication.* As we study the events of Scripture, let us be careful to listen to the whisper of the Holy Spirit as He applies the biblical record to our current reality. The Passion of Jesus is not just an event confined to history; it is an experience to be embraced in the lives of followers of Jesus Christ today. The historical events we will study have the potential and promise to give meaning to our current experience.

Finally, my prayer is that we would *desire more than an accumulation of information.* Instead, I pray that this study will bring life transformation. As you walk this journey, would you let Jesus lead you to a deeper understanding of the cross-centered life? With every step toward the cross, we will see glimpses of His love for us and His unfolding plan. As we walk in His steps, we remember that He said, "If anyone wants to come with Me, he must deny himself, take up his cross daily, and follow Me" (Luke 9:23).

Studying the cross is one thing, embracing it is quite another. As we begin the journey, it is important that we realize we do so with much more than an opportunity to learn facts about the last week of Jesus' life. While learning the facts is a good thing, it falls short of the ultimate goal. Keep in mind that the cross and resurrection are not just events to be remembered and studied. In fact, the writers of the New Testament consistently and wonderfully point us to the fact that these events open up a whole new world to those who actively trust in Jesus Christ.

Studying the cross is one thing, embracing it is quite another.

Our Savior—Jesus Christ

More than anything else, my hope and prayer is that this journey will lead us to a greater understanding of and intimacy with our Savior, Jesus Christ. With an awareness that His days on earth were coming to an end, Jesus' teaching and living in that last week were filled with an intensity of purpose and meaning that is unmatched in all of time. In our study, we will observe His actions, hear His teaching, experience His compassion, marvel at His courage, and most of all, be overwhelmed by His love. The events recorded in Jesus' final week on earth are both an *experience to be embraced* and *an example to be imitated*. Both aspects lead us to a deeper relationship with Him and a greater understanding of walking with Him.

Our Prayer

Take a moment to read through the hymn lyrics below as a personal prayer. May God use these words to prepare your heart for our journey with Jesus to the cross.

Lead Me to Calvary

King of my life, I crown Thee now,
Thine shall the glory be;
Lest I forget Thy thorn-crowned brow,
Lead me to Calvary.

Show me the tomb where Thou wast laid,
Tenderly mourned and wept;
Angels in robes of light arrayed
Guarded Thee whilst Thou slept.

Let me like Mary, through the gloom,
Come with a gift to Thee;
Show to me now the empty tomb,
Lead me to Calvary.

May I be willing, Lord, to bear
Daily my cross for Thee;
Even Thy cup of grief to share,
Thou hast borne all for me.

Lest I forget Gethsemane,
Lest I forget Thine agony;
Lest I forget Thy love for me,
Lead me to Calvary.[1]

[1] Words by Jennie E. Hussey, *The Worship Hymnal*, LifeWay, 2008, No. 251.

CHAPTER ONE

SUNDAY

The Journey Begins, The Mission Continues

LUKE 19:28-44

Our journey begins with Jesus' entry into Jerusalem—often called the triumphal entry—on the first day of the week. Quickly we recognize that we are not just walking on a journey with Jesus, we are seeing the Messiah on a mission. We join Him in the middle of what seems to have been a full and productive day. But before rushing to the scene of the celebration, let's take a moment to get our bearings. To fully appreciate the path we will walk with Jesus, we need to understand the purpose of His journey. Fortunately for us, there are significant mileposts that help us understand the mission of our Savior.

The most immediate context to understand are the events of that particular day. Luke's account suggests that Jesus began His day in Jericho with an encounter that would forever change the life of a tax collector named Zacchaeus (19:1-10). Following his encounter with the Messiah, this small-statured swindler was a changed man who was willing to put his money where his mouth was. The result was undeniable. Luke 19:8 records the powerful testimony of Zacchaeus, "Look, I'll give half of my possessions to the poor, Lord! And if I have extorted anything from anyone I'll pay back four times as much!" Jesus celebrated Zacchaeus' life-change and commitment with the affirming statement, "Today salvation has come to this house" (19:9). This powerful moment of celebration became the occasion for Jesus to state His life mission in a crystal clear statement: "For the Son of Man has come to seek and save the lost" (19:10). Before we go forward, let's take a few steps (or chapters) back to see Jesus' understanding of and commitment to His mission.

We need only go back one chapter to see that Jesus understood how seeking and saving the lost would involve a great sacrifice. In Luke 18:31-32, Jesus shared the following with His disciples:

> "Listen! We are going up to Jerusalem. Everything that is written through the prophets about the Son of Man will be accomplished. For He will be handed over to the Gentiles, and He will be mocked,

insulted, spit on; and after they flog Him, they will kill Him, and He will rise on the third day."

Above: Eastern (Golden) Gate in Jerusalem

Luke quickly added that the disciples did not understand what Jesus was saying to them (18:34), but Jesus was clear-eyed about what He was doing and why He was doing it. This was the third time in Luke's Gospel that Jesus predicted His death. The first two can be found in Luke 9:21-22 and Luke 9:43-44. All of these accounts give us the remarkable insight that Jesus knew the path He was walking. Some have explained this remarkable insight Jesus possessed and shared with His disciples as a "messianic consciousness," which can be simply explained as the awareness that He was the Messiah and had a unique mission to complete. Jesus not only understood this, He embraced

it wholeheartedly. Luke 9:51 further demonstrates Jesus' determination to fulfill the mission: "When the days were coming to a close for Him to be taken up, *He determined to journey* to Jerusalem" (emphasis added). A literal translation of "He determined to journey" could be, "He set His face to go to Jerusalem." Without question, Jesus was doggedly determined to embrace and fulfill His mission.

LEARNING ACTIVITY

Thanks for thinking of me ...

Review the paragraph below. Write a thank-you note to Jesus thanking Him for staying focused on His mission and what that means to you.

Jesus was willingly taking a road of sacrifice. As He walked the familiar road from Jericho toward Jerusalem that day, I wonder what He was thinking. Was He rejoicing over Zacchaeus' life change? Perhaps He thought about His disciples, ever by His side but often far away from His heart, and all that they needed to know in these moments. Maybe He thought of the crowds, like sheep without a shepherd, who would soon see

Left: The church at Bethphage that commemorates Christ mounting the donkey for His ride into Jerusalem on Palm Sunday

Far left: A stone inside the Bethphage sanctuary that tradition holds is the rock Christ stepped on to mount the donkey

that He was the great Shepherd willing to lay down His life for them. Maybe, just maybe, He thought about you and me. Though separated by centuries of time, He was walking the path to save us. While we do not know for certain what Jesus was thinking as He traveled the dusty path from Jericho to Jerusalem, I believe all of these are possibilities based on what we do know about His heart. As He approached the outskirts of Jerusalem, He was doing much more than travelling to a destination. He was forging a way for our eternal destiny.

The larger context of the story of the triumphal entry is recorded in Luke 19:28-44. Take a few moments to read the passage.

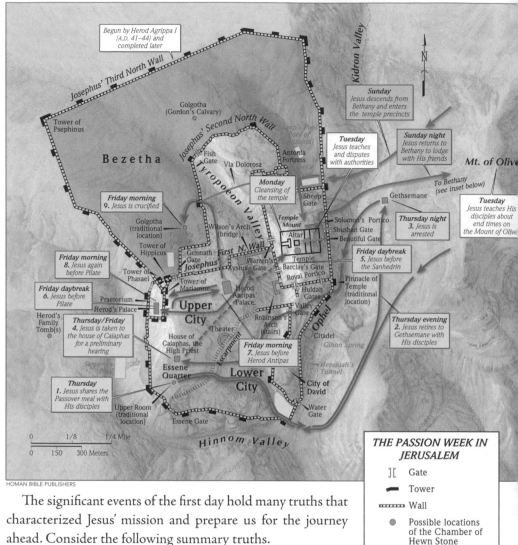

The significant events of the first day hold many truths that characterized Jesus' mission and prepare us for the journey ahead. Consider the following summary truths.

1. This moment was part of a deliberate and determined direction (Luke 19:31).

"If anyone asks you, 'Why are you untying it?' say this, 'The Lord needs it'" (19:31).

Jesus gave His disciples clear and careful instructions of where they were to go and what they were to seek. In this moment, Jesus again demonstrated His determination to walk the way of the cross. Though He was days away from the crucifixion, He was choosing to walk the journey. The events we will observe were not wasted moments of random events. Rather, Jesus approached this moment with deliberate actions and determined continuation.

2. This moment symbolizes a commitment of great cost (Luke 19:34-37a).

"Now He came near the path down the Mount of Olives" (19:37a).

Luke records that Jesus approached Jerusalem by way of the Mount of Olives (19:29), approaching the city from the East. As He topped the Mount of Olives, He would begin the sharp descent into a deep ravine called the Kidron Valley, separating the walled city of Jerusalem from the Mount of Olives.

When approaching the city from this direction, the temple complex would have dominated the landscape. Luke further records that it was precisely at the point where the road goes down the Mount of Olives (19:37) that Jesus rode the borrowed donkey colt.

There is much that could be said of this moment but we will limit our focus to two observations. The first is *Jesus' choice of transportation*. Rather than choosing an imposing stallion, Jesus chose a young donkey that had never been ridden (19:30). His choice illustrates both His humility and His awareness of His mission. His actions point to Zechariah's prophecy of the coming messiah (Zech. 9:9).

Below: Path to Bethany from Jerusalem

The second observation involves *the topography of the path*. The path Jesus rode that day descended before it ascended (see Luke 19:37). The road would become a familiar path Jesus would use daily that week, entering the city and then finding respite outside the city walls in Bethany. Each day, the topography of the journey reminded Him that He must descend before He would ascend. In short, there was theology in the topography!

This was a journey that cost Jesus everything, but in turn established Him as Lord over all things. As we follow Christ on the journey, it will cost us everything, but He will bless us with all of who He is. Something of you must die so that something of God can live in you (see Luke 9:23).

ILLUSTRATOR PHOTO/ BOB SCHATZ (9/18/8)

3. This Messiah is a King with no rivals (Luke 19:36-40).

"I tell you, if they were to keep silent, the stones would cry out!" (19:40).

As Jesus came over the crest of the Mount of Olives, the crowds treated Him like the regal representative that He was, throwing their cloaks on the road (an act of homage and submission; see 2 Kings 9:13) and singing praises to the King (Luke 19:36-38). These attitudes and actions were reserved for royalty and were in full view of everyone. Perhaps even the watchful eyes of those who were crowded into the temple mount that day looked across the Kidron Valley at the display. At this point, the Pharisees in the crowd challenged Jesus, saying, "Teacher, rebuke Your disciples." To which Jesus replied, "I tell you, if they were to keep silent, the stones would cry out!" (19:40). Every time I read those words I think of a song that I heard years ago that goes something like this, "Ain't no rock gonna take my place!" That isn't great grammar, but it is great theology. The path to the cross gives evidence to the praise that is due the King of kings.

It is worth pointing out how certain religious groups have come to view the Kidron Valley. The Kidron Valley is also known as the Valley of Jehosophat (mentioned only in Joel 3:2 and 3:12), and has come to be identified by both Muslims and Jews as the site of Jehovah's final judgment. Hundreds, if not thousands, of grave sites of both Jews and Muslims line the slopes of the valley. As Christians, we believe there will be a final judgment—one in which Jesus will be seen as the King with no rivals. Perhaps one day, the very place where Jesus was received and praised as king will be the place where He is revealed to be the King of kings and Lord of lords.

4. His actions present us with a decision that matters (Luke 19:41-44).

"Because you did not recognize the time of your visitation" (19:44b).

Surrounded by the cries of praise and encircled by a regal reception, Jesus looked over the city of Jerusalem and was reminded that He was going to be a king like no other. He was not just coming as a reigning king, He was coming as the Suffering Servant. He recognized that what He was coming to do would not be accepted by all. In this poignant moment, Jesus looked over Jerusalem and wept that so many would reject Him and the mission He came to fulfill. He saw not only the rejection, but the heart-breaking consequences of that rejection.

Jesus prophetically and accurately described the coming fall of Jerusalem (Luke 19:43-44). He described in astonishing detail what would happen some 40 years later when Jerusalem was destroyed in 70 A.D. He wept over the fact that His love would be rejected by many and He spoke directly to the reason of their rejection: they did not recognize the moment that Jesus visited them. Tragically, many in Jerusalem would reject the Messiah who humbly rode into their lives that Sunday afternoon. May we not miss the opportunity for King Jesus to do a work in our lives.

Questions for the Journey

1. What evidence most convinces you that Jesus recognized He was the Messiah and that He had a mission to complete?

2. To complete the mission, Jesus made a great commitment. For you to follow Christ on the journey, what in you must die so that He can live fully in you?

3. Are you living a life of worship acknowledging that Jesus is the King with no rivals?

4. What competing loves and loyalties in your life need to be dethroned so that Jesus can take full control of your life?

5. What decisions do you need to make today to follow Jesus fully?

6. What is the first or next step you need to take to join Jesus on the journey, and when will you take it?

CHAPTER TWO

MONDAY

Cleaning Out the Clutter

LUKE 19:45-46

One of my favorite Easter messages contains a line that is repeated throughout the sermon: "It's Friday, but Sunday is coming!" The obvious reference is that things might look bad on Friday when Jesus is nailed to the cross, but just wait, resurrection is coming! What a great line! A friend of mine who was familiar with the phrase altered it a bit to describe the difference between a powerful day of worship on Sunday and the reality of life that often hits on Monday morning. "It's Sunday, but Monday is coming!"

Such is the reality of life. Some days we start by saying, "Good morning, Lord!" Other days we start by saying, "Good Lord, it's morning." I'm not sure which of these two categories you fall into most often, but I am definitely more the latter. Monday mornings are

---

LEARNING ACTIVITY

It feels like a Monday

Imagine you are at work on Monday morning and you have made your list for the week. Your schedule is busy but it looks as if you are going to have a productive and successful week. Nothing is going to keep you from accomplishing your plans. Suddenly your boss comes in and asks to review your plans. He looks at you and states that you are working on the wrong projects and your priorities are wrong. You have to decide what you need to give up or quit doing and refocus on more important work.

How would you feel?

How would you respond?

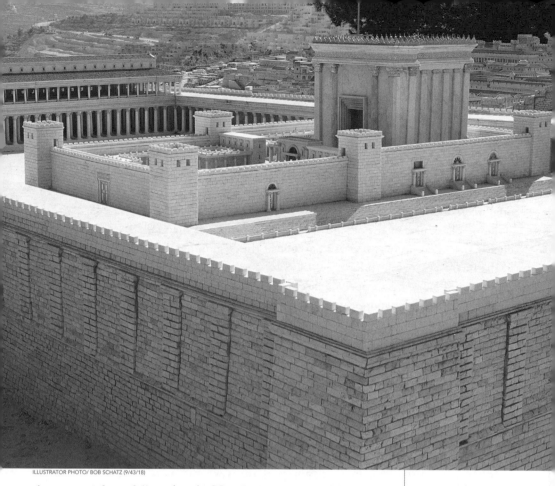

the worst. After a full weekend of family experiences and ministry opportunities, I am much more likely on Monday morning to want to sleep in than to charge out to take on the world.

As we continue on our journey with Jesus to the cross, Monday is a unique day. The only event recorded about Monday has been described as the cleansing of the temple. For those who are most comfortable with a meek and mild Jesus, this day of the journey will stretch your understanding of Him. When I read Luke's account of Monday in Jesus' last week, I almost feel justified in my Monday mood! Unfortunately, before I can claim biblical grounds for my manic Mondays, I have to dig a little deeper to understand what was happening the Monday of the greatest week in history.

Luke's account of Monday is simple and succinct. In fact, it is somewhat difficult to detect that the account of the triumphal entry and the cleansing of the temple are on different days. Take a moment to read Luke 19:45-46.

Above: A model of the temple at the Holyland Hotel, Jerusalem

He went into the temple complex and began to throw out those who were selling, and He said, "It is written, My house will be a house of prayer, but you have made it a den of thieves!"

The other Gospel writers help us to round out our understanding. They describe a similar cleansing of the temple (Matt. 21:12-19; Mark 11:12-19; John 2:13-22). Matthew and Mark's accounts make it clear that this event occurred on Monday of the final week of Jesus' life and ministry.

John's placement of the account is at the beginning of his Gospel, leading some to believe that there were two cleansings, one at the beginning of Jesus' ministry and one in the final week of His ministry. Others have suggested that John's account is placed at the beginning of his Gospel for theological purposes. They would say that the event happened where the Synoptic writers have placed it, but John used the story as an illustration of how Jesus was making all things new. Both of these explanations are plausible, but I find the former to be preferable. Regardless, the importance of this event is far greater than the number of times it happened. The importance has to do with Jesus' actions in relationship to the primary place of worship, the temple.

Understanding the Temple: A Place of Worship

For many years I completely misunderstood the importance of this story. Most of my childhood was spent living in Mississippi and Texas where I worshiped with my family in small to mid-size churches. When I heard the story of Jesus' cleansing the temple, I always envisioned Jesus walking into the foyer of the church or maybe even down to the front row of the church and taking on the ushers while the whole church watched. It was not that the ushers were doing anything wrong (in fact, they were some of the most likeable people at church), I just had a hard time understanding exactly what Jesus was doing.

Much of my misunderstanding had to do with my lack of appreciation for what the temple represented and my lack of awareness about the size and scale of the temple complex. Since I might not be alone in my misunderstanding, I will take a moment to briefly clarify what I have come to understand about the temple before we take a closer look at this symbolic step in Jesus' journey to the cross.

The temple was central to the Jews' worship in Jesus' day. For those living in Jerusalem, it was a major part of the city's religious, social, and even economic life. For Jews living outside Jerusalem, the temple represented a place they would strive to return to as often as possible, especially in the major moments of celebration. The week we are focusing on was the week of the Passover celebration, the Jewish feast celebrating God's deliverance from the tyranny of Pharaoh and the bitterness of slavery. The temple would

ILLUSTRATOR PHOTO/ DAVID ROGERS/ MUSEUM OF ART AND ARCHAEOLOGY/ UNIVERSITY OF MISSOURI/ COLUMBIA (407/24)

Above: Bronze incense shovel from Israel

have been packed with people in a city overflowing with as many as a million people.

The temple complex in Jesus' day was an impressive and massive area. The actual complex was made up of approximately 35 acres. The temple had been under construction under the direction of King Herod for 46 years and was elaborately constructed and beautifully adorned. The complex consisted not only of the temple itself, but many spacious and beautiful porticoes that surrounded it and provided areas for people to gather. When entering the complex there were a series of elevated terraces, each rising higher, with the temple as the highest point.

The actual temple was 150 feet high and 90 feet wide, with an elaborate porch surrounding the exterior. It was built of white marble, adorned with large plates of gold in the front that gleamed in the midday sun. Josephus, a first-century historian, compared the beautiful marble structure to a snow-covered mountain. The interior of the temple consisted of two main rooms: the holy place and the most holy place (often called the holy of holies). These two rooms were divided by a large curtain that separated the outer holy place from the inner room of the most holy place. The most holy place was entered only once a year by the high priest, and he would come only with the blood of a sacrifice, symbolizing the covering of his sins and the sins of the people. A thorough explanation of this sacrifice is beyond the scope of the current study, but the significance of this space was central in the whole of the temple complex. The most holy place was where the ark of the covenant was originally located and, in the Old Testament, had been designated as the place from which God reigned. However, by New Testament times the holy of holies was empty because the ark of the covenant along with its contents had been taken during the Babylonian conquest of Jerusalem in 587 B.C.

The outer room, the holy place, was an area where priests could come and go daily in their service of the sacrificial system. This room contained the altar of incense, the table of sacred bread (called Shewbread), and the seven-branched golden candlestands called *menorah*.

A CLOSER LOOK
The Temple Complex

Outside the actual temple building were a number of courtyards clearly designated for certain groups of people to enter or to avoid. The courtyard area closest to the temple building, just outside the holy place, was *the court of the priests*. This was the area containing the laver (a large basin used for ceremonial washing) and the altar where sacrifices were made. This area could be accessed only by priests. In close proximity was *the court of Israel*. All that happened in the court of priests was easily observed from this court because of the close proximity and the elevation difference. Only Jewish men were able to come into the court of Israel. This large courtyard was the site of worship, prayer, singing, reading of Scripture, and the continual sacrifices of animals on the altar. Interestingly, a priest offering a sacrifice with his back toward the temple could look forward out over the Kidron Valley and see across to the Mount of Olives.

Further back from this area was *the court of women*, a courtyard where Jewish women could come to worship. While the women could not enter the area designated for the men, they could see all that was occurring.

Even further from this area was *the court of the Gentiles*. This was the area of the temple where non-Jews could come to the temple for worship, prayer, or perhaps simply to observe. They could stand at a distance to watch, listen, and even participate, but they could not go beyond the very clear barrier delineating their proper place. This designated area for the Gentiles bled over into the remainder of the actual temple mount. This area was the size of four football fields and was surrounded by porches and porticoes. In addition, there were many entrances and exits that were used for access to the temple, but also were used as shortcuts for those passing through Jerusalem. The area for the Gentiles had become a place for local merchants to set up shop to provide animals that could be purchased for sacrifice or to exchange foreign currencies for the acceptable coinage needed to give offerings in the coffers of the temple. During the major Jewish celebrations such as Passover and the Week of Unleavened Bread, which preceded the Passover, the temple complex would be filled with thousands, if not hundreds of thousands, of people. The area designated for the Gentiles

HEROD'S TEMPLE
(20 B.C.–70 A.D.)

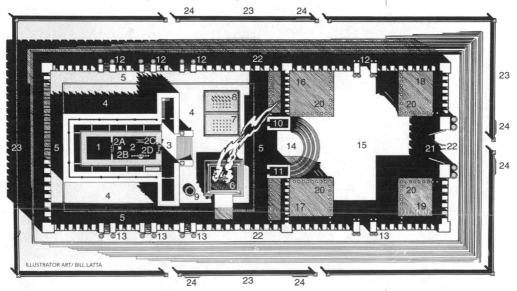

ILLUSTRATOR ART/ BILL LATTA

1. Holy of Holies	7. Animal Tethering Area	15. Court of Women
2. Holy Place	8. Slaughtering and Skinning Area	16. Nazirites' Court
2a. Veil	9. Laver	17. Wood Storage
2b. Altar of Incense	10. Chamber of Phineas	18. Lepers' Court
2c. Table of Shew Bread	11. Chamber of the Bread Maker	19. Oil Storage
2d. Great Menorah	12. North Gates	20. Women's Balconies
3. Temple Porch	13. South Gates	21. Gate Beautiful
4. Court of Priests	14. Nicanor Gate	22. Terrace
5. Court of Israel		23. Soreg
6. Altar of Burnt Offerings		24. Gentile Warning Inscriptions

was congested and commercialized. In addition, there were those who would abuse the needs of worshipers, apparently charging high prices or rates of return for the religious services they were providing. Instead of being a place of worship, the temple had become a profit center for those who would take advantage of the needs of worshipers.

Understanding The Cleansing of the Temple

With this in mind we return to Luke's succinct account of how Jesus responded to what was occurring in the temple. He said, "It is written, My house will be a house of prayer, but you have made it a den of thieves!" (Luke 19:46).

Luke's account of the cleansing of the temple had several purposes. First, it introduces the temple as the major setting for Luke's Passion Narrative. In Luke 19:47 we are told: "Every day He was teaching in the temple complex."

Second, the temple represents the focal point for the escalating tensions between Jesus and the religious leaders. Luke 19:47 highlights these growing tensions that would ultimately lead to Jesus' trial and crucifixion: "The chief priests, the scribes, and the leaders of the people were looking for a way to destroy Him."

Third, the temple became a place where people could hear the truth of God's plan and purpose. Luke 19:48 demonstrates that though the religious leaders desired to destroy Jesus, "they could not find a way to do it because all the people were captivated by what they heard." Jesus was restoring God's original intent for the temple, a place to meet with and to hear from God.

A final purpose fits into the larger message of the gospel and Jesus' mission. The cleansing of the temple was a small example of the cleansing work of Christ on the cross. Jesus would do whatever it took to invite all people into relationship with the Father. Anything less is a counterfeit and will not be tolerated. This final purpose is made clear when we read Mark's account in Mark 11:15-19. Take a moment to read this passage. Keep in mind this incident did not occur in isolation, but was a part of a larger lesson Jesus was teaching on Monday.

Mark's account includes the story of the cursing of the fig tree (Mark 11:12-14, 20-21). The cursing of the fig tree and the explanation of that event are like bookends around Mark's account of the cleansing of the temple and show that in Mark's presentation, the two events are complementary. Just as Jesus cursed a fig tree full of leaves but lacking fruit, He was cleansing a temple full of religious activity but lacking real relationships with the Father. Jesus looked beyond the leaves of religious activity and looked for the reality of the fruit of righteousness that flows from a relationship with the Father. Instead of finding a genuine place of worship, He found an empty imitation.

Jesus looked beyond the leaves of religious activity and looked for the reality of the fruit of righteousness that flows from a relationship with the Father.

Mark's account helps us see that Jesus not only spoke about the condition of His Father's house, but also began to take action. He threw out some people and overturned the tables of those turning a profit. Then He explained His actions in Mark 11:17: "Is it not written, 'My house will be called a house or prayer for all nations?' But you have made it a den of thieves!" His veiled message in the temple on Monday was that the good news that God's love is for all people. His clear message on the cross on Friday was that all are welcome to approach the Father. Luke 23:45 records

Left: A fig tree at Bethphage

that while Jesus was completing His mission on the cross, "the curtain of the sanctuary was split down the middle." What Jesus began in the cleansing of the temple, He completed by His work on the cross.

**What Jesus began in the cleansing of the temple,
He completed by His work on the cross.**

Practical Observations from the Cleansing of the Temple

1. True worship of God is centered in reality, not appearance.
2. Jesus expects fruit in our lives, especially when He sees leaves.
3. Religious activity doesn't automatically equal spiritual productivity. Be careful to discern the difference.
4. Empty religion builds barriers. God builds bridges.
5. Sin is serious and must be cleansed.
6. Jesus will confront people and places that misrepresent the heart of the Father.
7. Jesus will do what needs to be done.
8. The cross became the means by which we have access into the most holy place of God's presence.

Questions for the Journey
1. The New Testament teaches us that we are now the temple of God's presence (see 1 Cor. 6:19). Are there areas of your heart and life that need to be cleansed?

2. Studying Jesus' example in the temple, how should you respond when you see religious activity that misrepresents the heart of the Father?

3. Can you identify areas of religious activity in your life that lack spiritual productivity?

4. In your opinion, what is the significance of the cleansing of the temple in the overall picture of Jesus' last week on earth?

5. What is one specific way that you can go beyond superficial religious activity and center your life on Jesus this week? Consider these:
    * Set aside time to read the Gospel of Luke.
    * Give something generously and secretly, so as to reflect the spirit of Christ as opposed to the appearance of false religion.
    * Take the first step in mending a broken relationship, regardless of who is at fault.

6. Why is long-term fruitfulness and purity more satisfying than superficial, religious appearance?

7. Name one time when you did the best thing as opposed to the religious thing and describe how it felt.

CHAPTER THREE

TUESDAY AND WEDNESDAY
The Issue Is Authority

LUKE 20–21

*One day as He was teaching the people in the temple complex and
proclaiming the good news, the chief priests and the scribes, with the
elders, came up and said to Him: "Tell us, by what authority are You
doing these things? Who is it who gave You this authority?"*
(Luke 20:1-2)

Authority is a major issue in our world today. All of us are faced with issues of authority. Whether you are on the ball field, in the boardroom, at the schoolhouse, or at your house, the need for authority is present. When I think of the issue of authority, a well-known illustration comes to mind.

The captain of a battleship was navigating through treacherous waters on a dark night when he noticed a light ahead that appeared to be another vessel. In order to avert disaster, he quickly radioed: "Advise you change course 20 degrees to avoid collision."

Back came the reply: "Advise you change *your* course 20 degrees."

Again the captain radioed: "I'm a captain, change your course 20 degrees."

"I'm a seaman," came the reply, "you had better change *your* course 20 degrees."

Angered and frustrated that this disrespectful seaman was endangering the lives of his crew, the captain shouted: "I am a battleship! Change your course 20 degrees!"

Back came the reply: "I'm a lighthouse."

End of discussion. The battleship changed course.

Unfortunately, the issue of ultimate authority is not always so easily established. In these days of tolerance, there appears to be an unending attempt to diminish or blur the distinctives of the Christian faith. Ultimate authority is viewed with skepticism. Beliefs are often challenged, calling into question the authority behind the beliefs that are held. Then there is the problem of a general lack of integrity. There are many examples of this, but it is most clearly seen when a public figure professes to adhere to a certain belief system but then fails to live by those beliefs. When news of a disconnect

between professed beliefs and private behaviors comes to light, the authority of the person is greatly diminished or discredited. Interestingly enough, the attack often goes beyond the person's weakness to the very beliefs themselves. The underlying issue is the authority of the person, his beliefs, and his behaviors. We

Above: The Moslem Dome of the Rock sits on the Temple Mount where Herod's Temple once stood.

My Authorities

In the space below, list those who you consider to have authority over you. If you were asked to go on a dangerous mission to rescue someone, which of these authorities would you follow? Check the box of those you would trust. Why?

☐ _____

☐ _____

☐ _____

☐ _____

☐ _____

☐ _____

ILLUSTRATOR ART/ BILL LATTA

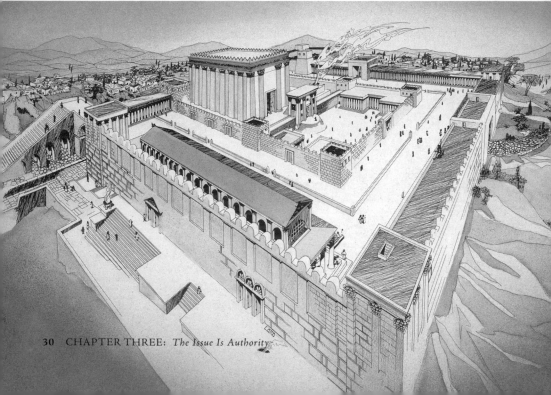

live in a world that needs an authority to recognize, trust, and yield to.

Fortunately for followers of Christ, we have found the One who has ultimate authority. The events of Tuesday and Wednesday highlight the claim that Jesus has ultimate authority. He has the authority to be both our Savior and Lord. As Savior, He has the authority to forgive our sins and to redeem our lives. As Lord, He is worthy of our love, our ultimate loyalty, and our accountability of how we live our everyday lives. To be led, we must be willing to allow another to have control of our lives. Christ's leadership in our lives flows from our belief that He has the authority to be the Lord of our lives. We should not be surprised that this is controversial to those who do not share our beliefs, nor should we be ignorant or arrogant regarding those who are unaware of why we embrace the authority of Jesus. Rather, we have determined that Jesus Christ is worthy to have authority in our lives and we invite others to experience the same in their lives.

In our study at hand, we see how Jesus responded to the challenges and questions regarding His authority. Days three and four of our journey with Jesus to the cross were filled with questions, controversy, and rising tensions. Chapters 20 and 21 of Luke record Jesus' teaching in the temple over the period of several days, which probably included Tuesday and Wednesday. Some of Jesus' teaching might have taken place at a different location like the Mount of Olives, but this information is not provided by Luke. Luke's narrative begins (20:1-2) and ends (21:37-38) with summary statements about the effectiveness of Christ's teaching and the receptiveness of the people.

Luke 21:37-38 describes what seems to be the daily schedule on Tuesday and Wednesday of that week:

> During the day, He was teaching in the temple complex, but in the evening He would go out and spend the night on what is called the Mount of Olives. Then all the people would come early in the morning to hear Him in the temple complex.

Above: Silver shekels of the city of Tyre, 1st century A.D. Religious taxes, such as those Jews gave at the temple at Jerusalem, were paid in the main silver coin in Judea, the shekel of Tyre.

Lower left: Artist's redition of Herod's temple complex in Jerusalem

Luke did not elaborate on the specific moments of respite each night, though Matthew and Mark allow us to see how these challenging days of teaching ended with less public moments in Bethany (Matt. 26:6 and Mark 14:3). Luke instead chose to focus on the intensification of conflict with the religious leaders. Luke 19:47-48 shows how many of the people were captivated by Jesus' teaching, but those in the religious establishment were infuriated. After Jesus' cleansed the temple and challenged those in charge, the wheels of conflict that would ultimately end with the crucifixion were set in motion.

With the passing of each day of the greatest week in history, the conflict intensified between those who did not accept Jesus, His teaching, or the One who sent Him. Like so many other moments in Jesus' ministry, His teaching was captivating to those who trusted Him and polarizing to those who did not. The teachings recorded in Luke 20 and 21 represent a broad spectrum of topics. Some topics were initiated by Jesus, but most were answers to questions that were presented to Jesus as a challenge. The following is an outline of the material contained within these two chapters.

Luke 20:1-2   Jesus' Authority Questioned
Luke 20:2-8   Jesus Questions the "Authorities" about John the Baptist's Baptism
Luke 20:9-19   The Parable of the Tenants and the Rising Tension with the Religious Leaders

Left: A tomb of the Sanhedrin in Jerusalem. The Sanhedrin was the governing body of the Jews in the Greek and Roman periods. It consisted of 70 members plus its leader, the high priest.

Each of these sections could represent an individual chapter of our study and are certainly worthy of further study. For our purposes, we will focus only on the parable of the tenants found in Luke 20:9-19 and Jesus' message about being ready in Luke 21:34-36. A summary of key lessons, some drawn from the passages above, will conclude the chapter.

The Parable of the Tenants—A Parable of Authority (Luke 20:9-19)

Jesus often chose to teach through parables. Although parables do not explicitly state the lesson intended for the audience, the method in which the story is delivered leaves little room for the overall message to be misinterpreted. In other words, Jesus was speaking directly to the people in a way that allowed them to see for themselves the truths He told.

The parable of the tenants had a clear meaning for all who were listening, especially the religious leaders. Throughout the Old Testament and in the collective historical consciousness of Israel was likened to a vineyard prepared by God. Jesus recounted how the owner rented his vineyard to tenant farmers, allowing them to enjoy the fruits of the harvest, but expecting them to be grateful stewards. At harvest time, he sent various servants with the expectation that they would provide fruit for the owner.

Surprisingly, the tenant farmers did not send the servants back with any fruit. Instead, in various ways they treated the servants harshly and shamefully, dishonoring both the servants and the owner. The situation became so tenuous that the owner decided to send his beloved son in the hopes that the tenants would respect the authority represented in the presence of the son. In an astonishing display of disrespect, the tenants, driven by their misguided greed, threw the son out of the vineyard and killed him. Without question, this parable must have drawn a gasp from those listening. This was a blatant and almost unthinkable display of dishonor.

Then Jesus said, "Therefore, what will the owner of the vineyard do to them? He will come and destroy those farmers and give the vineyard to others" (20:15-16).

The crowd could hardly believe what they were hearing and could not contain themselves. They cried, "No—never!" Jesus replied with a question about the meaning of Psalm 118:22. He then answered the question Himself (20:18) and effectively declared Himself the Son who was sent to Israel. Jesus was declaring Himself to be the stone that the builders would reject but that would become the chief cornerstone. Luke did not record whether the people understood what Jesus was saying, but he did record that the scribes and chief priests understood very clearly what Jesus was saying. Luke noted that they were so angry they "looked for a way to get their hands on Him that very hour, because they knew He had told this parable against them, but they feared the people" (20:19). They understood Jesus' teaching but did not yield to His authority.

LEARNING ACTIVITY

A Modern Day Parable of Authority

Read Luke 20:9-19. Use the parable to create a modern-day version that illustrates the principles Jesus was sharing. Refer to information in this learner guide for ideas.

The Need for Watchfulness: Living Under Authority
(Luke 21:34-36)

In contrast to those who challenged and rejected Jesus' authority, Jesus taught those willing to live under His authority to be watchful and ready. After prophetically speaking about the things to come (21:7-33), Jesus exhorted His disciples to live with a constant awareness of these ultimate realities. His words reveal His astute awareness that we all, in varying degrees, can become distracted from or completely oblivious to God's continually unfolding plan (21:34). To avoid the trap of complacency, Jesus called His followers to lives of commitment, courage, and consistency. This type of dependent, humble living was in sharp contrast to the defensiveness and defiance of those opposing Jesus' teaching.

Summarizing Tuesday and Wednesday

So, how does all of this fit into the big picture of our journey to the cross? What is it that we need to understand, observe, and embrace? I would summarize the events of Tuesday and Wednesday with three statements. The first two will be easily seen. The third will require a brief look just beyond the section of Scripture that we have been considering, but quite possibly within the events of Tuesday and Wednesday.

First, our study reveals that over these two days *opposition increased and authority was the issue.* A second observation is that *communication intensified and clarity was the response.* Jesus was very clear with His critics and opponents. The third observation is that during this time *devotion was invited but deception was often the reality.* Different people responded in different ways but those who rejected Jesus rarely did so openly. They were not forthright about their feelings or faith in regard to Jesus.

I am so struck by this final dynamic that occurred in that week. Clearly, the heart of Jesus was to invite His hearers to receive His love and His leadership. Some responded with devotion. Others despised Him and plotted to destroy Him. Still others were deceptive, publicly following Him but privately planning to betray Him. The relational dynamics of these two days would be another interesting study, but consider this one thought: *One person's act of devotion became the catalyst for another's act of betrayal.* Matthew and Mark record that as Jesus retreated to Bethany on Wednesday night an unnamed lady anointed Him with expensive perfume (Matt. 26:6-13; Mark 14:3-10). This beautiful display of devotion was controversial among Jesus' disciples. While Jesus defended and applauded this extravagant act of worship, the occasion seems to have been the moment when one of the Twelve, Judas Iscariot, decided to betray Jesus. Luke 22:1-5 records the moment that the destructive desires of the religious leaders combine with the duplicitous heart of Judas. This moment of striking contrast will lead to the next step and stage in our journey. All of these dynamics might have been overwhelming to Jesus, but He knew all things.

Then, as now, it is clear that how you are living your life clearly identifies who is leading your life. May we be granted the grace and given the strength to live under His lordship in our lives.

Observations and Applications

The following are some general observations and applications from the passages we have been studying:

+ Jesus knew that the authority of the Father and the Son would be challenged before it would be displayed (Luke 20:9-18).
+ Jesus used His authority to serve and lead others, not to dominate or abuse others (Luke 22:24-27).
+ Jesus' responses to the challenges and attacks of His authority are a powerful example of how we can stand courageously and graciously against those who oppose Him.
+ Jesus' teaching and interaction with His enemies were small examples of His ultimate act of service at the cross.
+ Jesus will come again in ultimate and unchallenged authority (Luke 21:27).
+ Before Jesus comes again, the continued rejection of His authority will lead to difficult times in the world and in the lives of believers (Luke 21:25-26).
+ We will face persecution from those who deny the authority of Jesus (Luke 21:12-19).
+ We should anchor our hope in Jesus' promise that we are secure in Him (Luke 21:18-19,28,36).
+ Until He comes, we must live our lives constantly vigilant, watchful, alert, prayerful, humble, and dependent on His power (Luke 21:34-36).
+ Different responses to Jesus do not diminish His authority, but they do decide the destiny of those responding.

Questions for the Journey

1. What is the visible evidence in your life that Jesus is your ultimate authority?

2. Do you see examples of how the authority of Jesus is challenged, ignored, or undermined in our culture?

3. Based on the example of Jesus, how should you respond to the challenges to Jesus' authority today? (Think about the different ways Jesus responded over the course of two days and apply them to your life and situation.)

4. How can you put into practice this week Jesus' instructions in Luke 21:34-36 regarding how to live until He returns?

5. Do you think that being a follower of Christ, as discussed in this chapter, is a privilege or a task? Explain your answer.

CHAPTER FOUR

THURSDAY

A Day and Night of Major Messages

LUKE 22:7-65

Then the Day of Unleavened Bread came when the Passover lamb had to be sacrificed. Jesus sent Peter and John saying, "Go and prepare the Passover meal for us, so we can eat it"
(Luke 22:7-8).

Several years ago, I heard a friend and mentor of mine talking about the importance of saying what needs to be said to those whom we love the most. As I listened to him talk, I started identifying the thoughts in my head and the feelings that I had in my heart that I had never found a way to express clearly to those I love the most. Since then, I have tried to periodically hit the pause button of life and make myself identify the major messages I want my family and closest friends to hear clearly from me, whether in print or in person. I have found with every passing season of life, there are both recurring themes and brand new thoughts I need to express clearly. I need to capture these thoughts, and those I love need to hear them from me. Sometimes my thoughts are about my love and appreciation. Other times they are core beliefs I hold dearly that I want them to know and embrace. Sometimes there are observations of their lives and living that I admire and want to make sure they know I have seen and appreciate. Every one of us needs this kind of life-focusing discipline that results in life-giving communication and affirmation.

On a recent trip to the Ukraine, I was reminded I had not taken the time to do this in my family for some time. I was travelling with a friend to spend a week teaching and preaching in the Odessa region of that beautiful country. Specifically, I had been asked to teach the Pastoral Letters (1 and 2 Timothy and Titus) at the Odessa Theological Seminary. While somewhere over the Atlantic Ocean, I was moved to tears as I read 2 Timothy. I thought about the seasoned apostle Paul writing what he knew was very likely his last message to his son in the ministry. This thought, along with my fear of flying and strong turbulence, made me start thinking about my own kids. What if I had spoken to them for the last time? Had I spoken into their lives clearly about the

big picture of my hopes and desires for their lives? If they had heard their last message from me, would they have understood all that I wanted and needed them to hear? Fortunately, I had the opportunity to express some of those thoughts to them with my safe arrival home. However, once again I was reminded of the importance of making sure that the major messages of life are communicated.

Above: The Upper Room, or the Hall of the Coenaculum, was restored in the 14th Century using antique columns and capitals and adding the Gothic vaulted ceiling. The stone flooring is possibly from the original building.

ILLUSTRATOR PHOTO/ BOB SCHATZ (16/27/16)

ILLUSTRATOR PHOTO/ BRENT BRUCE/ UNIVERSITY OF PENNSYLVANIA MUSEUM OF ARCHAEOLOGY AND ANTHROPOLOGY (32/43/18)

LEARNING ACTIVITY

My Life Messages

Compile a list of life messages you desire to communicate to others through your actions, attitudes, and words.

After reading Luke's record of that Thursday in the greatest week in history, I couldn't stop thinking the words *major messages*. With every step that Jesus walked closer to the cross, He was compelled to clarify and magnify the major messages of His life and mission. In these intense, last moments of communication, He would reveal even more about how His life mission was a continuation of His Father's plan of redemption. Like the last words of a father to his children, Jesus made His life message clear. Although clearly communicated, His message was not fully comprehended or appreciated. With each passing day in the greatest week in history, carrying out His mission grew increasingly more difficult. Thursday was no exception as Jesus made clear His life message of love against the backdrop of the shared Passover, one of Israel's biggest celebrations. Beyond that, He elaborated on the message by a season of soul-searching surrender and accentuated it by a tenacious grace in the face of betrayal and denial.

Take a moment to read Luke's account of Thursday in Luke 22:7-71. Be sure to listen for the major messages in the events of the day and late into the night.

Above: Egyptian scarab of Thutmose III, who ruled 1479-1425 B.C. The translation of the inscription reads, "Establisher of the form of Ra." Thutmose III was likely the pharaoh of the exodus.

Left: Workman's village at Medinet Habu, Egypt. Workman (or slaves) may have lived in this complex.

Inset left: This slightly larger than life size head was part of a standing statue of one of Egypt's most powerful rulers, Thutmosis III.

The Message of the Passover Preparation (Luke 22:7-13)

Luke described Thursday as "the day of Unleavened Bread … when the Passover lamb had to be sacrificed" (22:7). The story of the original Passover event is recorded in Exodus 11–12. The Passover celebration annually commemorated the historical moment when God intervened in a powerful way to deliver His people from the brutality of Pharaoh's rule and the bondage of slavery in Egypt. For 400 years, the Israelites had been held in bondage in Egypt until God intervened.

The account recorded in Exodus both described the historical occasion of the Passover and prescribed for coming generations the proper way to celebrate God's redemption. The celebration of Passover was preceded by a period of preparation called the Festival of Unleavened Bread (referred to in Luke 22:1). During these days, the leaven, often seen as a symbol of sin, was removed from the homes of Jewish celebrants. It was a process of purification with spiritual and practical applications. Spiritually, it reminded the Israelites and their descendants that they were to be a holy people, set apart to God. Practically, it prepared the Israelites to be ready to travel quickly. They would not have time to wait on the bread to rise and would need to be ready at the moment when God acted. Anticipation of God's continued redemptive purposes personified in the promise of the Messiah was and is a major theme for the Jews. As believers, we believe Jesus is the Messiah bringing full meaning to this aspect of the Passover.

All of this preparation would lead to the actual Passover celebration. In days preceding the historical Passover event, as the Israelites had been preparing themselves, God was working to confront Pharaoh. After a series of nine different plagues on Egypt, Pharaoh stubbornly refused to release the Israelites. God then prepared the Israelites for the tenth and final plague, the death of the first born of all Egypt. The Lord promised the Jewish people that the death angel would pass over their homes if they killed an unblemished lamb, or a young goat, and painted the door frame of their homes with the blood. That night, Egypt was filled with grief while the Hebrews were filled with awe. Pharaoh ordered the Israelites to go and they hurriedly slipped into their freedom.

Each year the Jewish people played out this drama of God's redemption in the Passover celebration. Fifteen hundred years after that event, Jesus came to Jerusalem to observe the Passover with His disciples. They would join the throngs of pilgrims, hundreds of thousands of them, who would press into Jerusalem to celebrate.

Notice how Jesus made careful preparation for the Passover celebration with His disciples (22:7-13). Ironically, while He was making preparation for the disciples, one of His disciples was making preparations to participate in a plan with the religious authorities that would lead to Jesus' death. For a price of 30 pieces of silver, Judas agreed to betray Jesus (22:5-6). Warren Wiersbe commented on this moment, saying, "It is incredible that these men perpetrated history's greatest crime during Israel's holiest festival."[1] In the middle of this trauma and turmoil, there was the clear-eyed and calm-spirited Messiah. He was prepared and kept leading His disciples forward.

The Message of the Passover Celebration (Luke 22:14-16)

The emotions of the evening already were high because of the celebration itself, and the disciples must have been both excited and anxious as Jesus spoke. His words show the intensity of this moment and His feelings for the disciples. In Luke 22:15-16 He said, "I have fervently desired to eat this Passover with you before I suffer. For I tell you, I will not eat it again until it is fulfilled in the kingdom of God." Jesus would then proceed to share the powerful message of God's continued redemptive activity, giving new meaning to the Passover meal.

The Passover meal was the central moment in the celebration. Through an established order of events called a *seder* (meaning "order"), the meal would assist the Jews in recounting the story of their redemption. Everything was to be done in order, and every step was rich in symbolism. The meal would have lasted for several hours and included relaxed moments of conversation and interaction.

A CLOSER LOOK
The Passover Seder

The equivalent in our experience might be a multiple course meal around the table at Thanksgiving or Christmas; though in our age of fast food and hurried dining, we are left with a somewhat shallow ability to understand the experience. This extended time is recounted by each of the Gospel writers in different ways. Luke's record is fairly succinct, but includes Jesus' revelation that someone would betray Him (vv. 21-22), His response to the disciples' debate about greatness (vv. 24-30), and some last words of preparation about the coming experience (vv. 35-38). All of this occurred in the context of the seder experience. John's Gospel provides an extended account of Jesus' teaching in John 13–17. For a fascinating study, read John 13–17 with the Passover seder in mind.

The meal was basically structured around the drinking of four symbolic cups. In addition to the cups there were other specific elements. There was unleavened bread, vegetables dipped in salt water signifying the tears that flowed as a result, a bitter mixture of herbs, a sweet mixture of fruit and honey that symbolized the sweetness of redemption, and the centerpiece of the meal—the lamb that had been sacrificed earlier in the day was consumed.

After an opening prayer, the designated leader began the experience with the first cup, *the cup of sanctification*. The participants were reminded they were to be a sanctified people. After they took the cup, everyone would get up and go to a place in the room where a basin filled with water would be provided to ceremonially wash their hands so that they would take the Passover with clean hands. This may have been the immediate context for the moment when Jesus would wash the disciples' feet described in John 13.

As the participants settled back around the table, the leader would take the vegetables and dip them in salt water to recount the years of slavery when the tears flowed. Then the leader would take the unleavened bread from a linen pouch, break it, and separate a larger piece to be hidden. This piece of bread would be "found" later in the meal. It was called the *afikomen*, which literally meant "that which is to come." The participants were to close their eyes as the bread was hidden somewhere around the table or the room. This kept the children involved in the long meal and would represent a powerful moment in the *seder*. This may have been the moment recorded in John 14 when Jesus told His disciples about going away and returning. Usually at this time someone at the table, typically a child, would ask, "Why are we eating this meal and why are we doing it this way?" This question would signal the preparation of the second cup, *the cup of deliverance*. Before partaking of the cup, there would be an extended recounting of God's deliverance from slavery, the dipping of bread into bitter herbs as a reminder of the slavery, quickly followed by the dipping of bread into the sweet mixture signifying the sweetness of deliverance. Then they would drink the second cup.

The lamb would be eaten next with the bread and vegetables. After the meal, the leader would announce that it was time for the *afikomen*. This was a fun moment as the participants would search for the hidden bread. There was the added excitement of knowing that the one who found the *afikomen* would be paid a gift, described as a ransom. The bread would be broken and shared among the group as a symbol of unity among them. They would then drink the third cup, *the cup of redemption*.

The final cup was *the cup of praise*. The leader would recount the story of Elijah who would come again and prepare the way for the coming of the messiah. In fact, the meal was eaten with the door open and a vacant place at the table as a tangible expression of the welcoming of the messiah. The meal would be completed with the drinking of this cup, followed by a psalm of praise.

Above: The Dormition Church on Mt. Zion in Jerusalem commemorates the site of the Last Supper.

The Message in the Last Supper (Luke 22:17-22)

It is in the context of the *seder* that we understand Jesus' words at the Last Supper. Luke records only two of the four cups (22:17,20), but it is clear that Jesus revealed His soon-to-be-place in the redemptive plan of God just as the *afikomen* was discovered and the cup of redemption was taken. He filled the meal with new meaning. The bread that was broken represented His body freely given for all. It would be a symbol to help the disciples remember. Jesus then took

ILLUSTRATOR PHOTO/ BRENT BRUCE (60/0182)

the cup and boldly stated He was establishing a new covenant, to be established by His own blood willingly poured out for all.

Though He never said it at the table, Jesus' actions demonstrated that He saw Himself as the Passover sacrifice. In new and greater ways He would provide sanctification, deliverance, redemption, and reason for praise. What was implicit in His actions at the table was made explicit by the writers of the New Testament. Jesus was the Passover Lamb of God (John 1:29), without blemish or defect (1 Peter 1:19), who was sacrificed for our sin (1 Cor. 5:7), who takes away the sin of the world (John 1:29), and will be forever praised for what He has done (Rev. 5:9-13). The disciples did not fully comprehend this message on that side of the cross, but in the hours that followed Jesus would demonstrate this message.

As Christians, we are often woefully unaware of the treasures of our spiritual heritage deeply rooted in God's redemptive work expressed in His covenant with Israel and recorded in the Old Testament. While Luke does not elaborate on these ideas, I would offer the following as points of praise to reflect on when we approach the table of our Lord to remember what He has done for us.

+ We have been delivered from the bitterness of bondage.
+ We have been sanctified by the blood of the Lamb.
+ We have been redeemed by the suddenness and sweetness of salvation.
+ We have experienced the fullness of forgiveness that fills our praise.

The Message of the Long Night (Luke 22:39-65)

"This is your hour—and the dominion of darkness" (Luke 22:53b).

The day was not yet done. After the Passover celebration, Jesus led His disciples out of Jerusalem and across the Kidron Valley to the Mount of Olives. At the table He foretold that on that very night He would be betrayed, denied, and would begin the long path of suffering that would ultimately lead to the cross. We find these events occurring just as Jesus predicted.

Jesus would leave the joy of the Passover celebration to embrace the agony of His mission. In the long night that was to follow, He would labor in excruciating prayer, looking squarely into the cup that He alone could drink (Luke 22:42). That which would bring life to us would first bring death to Him. We will never fully understand what happened in that moment of prayer as our Savior, with blood soaked brow, bowed to the will of Father and embraced the burden of our great need. On His knees, alone before the Father, Jesus once again communicated His consistent message. He surrendered to the will of His Father, accepting the cup and the cross that it represented. It was a long night, but it was not over.

Judas would betray Him with a kiss and Jesus' enemies would arrest Him (22:47-53). Peter would deny Him, and the soldiers

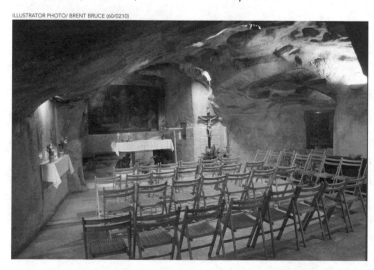

ILLUSTRATOR PHOTO/ BRENT BRUCE (60/0210)

Upper left: Garden at Gethsemane on the west slope of the Mount of Olives at Jerusalem

Left: The cave of Gethsemane. Gethsemane means olive oil press in Aramaic. This cave housed such a press. Since it is unlikely Jesus and the disciples were accustomed to sleeping outside, this cave may have served as their sleeping quarters.

would mock and beat Him (22:63-65). This was only the beginning of the brutality Jesus would endure, but the message was unmistakable. He would endure the pain of this path for the salvation of our souls.

We are not simply studying historical events; we are coming face-to-face with evidence of our great need and His great love.

A Personal Pause for Preparation for the Journey

As we come to this place in our study, instead of questions for the journey I would simply ask you to prepare yourself for the journey. Take a moment to reflect on some truths you learned from following Jesus on Thursday. In the space provided below, you might simply write down examples of the clear message of Jesus or insights that you will want to remember. Perhaps you would simply pray and then write down what you feel the Father is saying to you.

I must admit at this point in our journey I began to feel like a voyeur gazing upon actions of which I am unworthy to look. I am humbled, ashamed, and awed to know that the cup that Jesus embraced and the path that He would walk involved me. We are standing on the edge of a divine drama that will play out before us in the coming day. Friday will demonstrate unbelievable injustices and unspeakable atrocities for which we are indebted, but also responsible. Let us keep a humble heart and a holy awe. We are not simply studying historical events; we are coming face-to-face with evidence of our great need and His great love. Before we walk this path, would you bow a knee before your heavenly Father and pray the prayer of our Savior: "Not my will, but Yours be done."

LEARNING ACTIVITY

My Good News Message

Based on today's study, write a summary statement that describes the way you desire to reflect the message of the gospel in your life.

1. Warren Wiersbe, *The Bible Exposition Commentary: An Exposition of the New Testament Comprising the Entire "Be" Series, Volume 1* (Wheaton, Illinois: Victor Books, 1989) 264.

CHAPTER FIVE

FRIDAY

The Worst Good Day of History

LUKE 23:1-49

Our journey has been a powerful experience. As we have followed Jesus through the greatest week in history, we have seen and experienced triumphant praise, intense scrutiny, reverent receptivity, subtle and sinister challenge, staggering revelations, and from Jesus, constant commitment. Each step has taken us closer to the cross. Like travelling a winding mountain road through the forest, occasionally we have broken into a clearing to see the shape of something that lies beyond and above us. Yet, we have not yet seen the fullness of our destination. Today, we will see the cross.

It is Friday, a day that we now call "good," but only because what was accomplished that day will never have to be repeated again. Today, we will watch Jesus endure the petty political games of pitiful people. We will observe the senseless taunts, delivered unjustly by unworthy men. We will witness Jesus walk the cruel path of pain and sorrow, surrounded by people, but solely able to finish what had been started. Finally, we will see Him endure the brutal punishment reserved for the worst of criminals. He has prepared Himself for this moment. He has prepared us for this moment. Now, we will see the cross clearly.

Seeing the Cross Clearly

When you think of the cross, what comes to mind? Growing up as a preacher's kid meant that I had the opportunity to hear many sermons. Though my dad was a gifted preacher, and still is one of my favorites to hear, I must confess I can't remember a whole sermon outline from my early childhood years. While I don't remember an outline, I do remember the stories. My dad had a way of making the stories from the Bible memorable. In particular, I distinctly remember hearing the ones that surrounded the cross. I suppose it was during one of those messages that I began to try capturing what he was saying by sketching a picture in one of the blank pages at the front of my Bible. I don't remember if I finished the picture in one message, or if it was over the course of several,

but what I do know is the story of the cross was clear to me at the age of seven. Take a look at my attempt to capture the story of the cross.

Above: View of the exterior of the Church of the Holy Sepulcher

LEARNING ACTIVITY

At the Cross

As you look at the author's drawing of the cross at a young age, list words or describe feelings that come to mind.

I wasn't the greatest artist, but I did know the story. You will notice the crown of thorns, the sign above Jesus' head, the criminals on each side, and my attempt at a Roman soldier and Pharisees. I was particularly interested in the "spit," the jeering, and the spear that pierced Jesus' side.

Since then, I have learned much more about the cross. My understanding of the historical event and the theological meaning has been greatly expanded. I have heard sermons, read devotionals, seen movies, read and re-read the hundreds of Scriptures in both the Old and New Testament that describe the crucifixion of Jesus and explain all that the cross means. More importantly, I know the Savior who died on that cross. I am still moved by the moment when the Messiah willingly gave His life for you and for me. Each time I return to stand at the foot of the cross, I see it more clearly. As we continue our journey, my prayer is that we will see the cross more clearly than ever before.

More than any other symbol, the cross represents the Christian faith. While the empty tomb displays the work of our living Lord, the cross displays the sacrificial gift of our loving Savior. Many people wear a cross around their neck but do not understand its meaning in their lives. Before we rejoin Luke's account of Jesus' journey to the cross, I would offer a few thoughts to prepare us to see the cross clearly.

First of all, notice *the choice that Jesus made*. While the events of the day will reveal the manipulation and miscarriage of justice by religious and political leaders alike, these leaders did not ultimately make the choice. We will hear the cries from the crowd shouting, "Crucify Him! Crucify Him!" But remember, the crowds did not make the choice. We will see the cold and cruel work of the Roman soldiers as they callously carried out their charge to scourge and crucify Him, but the soldiers did not make the choice. No, Jesus chose the cross. Jesus said, "This is why the Father loves Me, because I am laying down My life so I may take it up again. *No one takes it from me, but I lay it down*, and I have the right to take it up again. I have received this command from My Father" (John 10:17-18, emphasis added). Jesus' death was no accident, it was an intentional choice. Remember, Jesus chose the cross.

Second, notice *the price Jesus paid*. The emotional, relational, and physical price Jesus paid was breathtaking and staggering. Even so, it pales in comparison to the spiritual price paid to deliver us from the debt of our sin. Jesus died to show us the stark sinfulness of sin. He went to the cross to demonstrate the horrific consequences of our sin we should have to experience, but that He would consume within Himself. Peter reflected on this reality when he wrote the following in 1 Peter 2:21-25:

> For you were called to this,
> because Christ also suffered for you,

leaving you an example,
so that you should follow in His steps.
He did not commit sin,
and no deceit was found in His mouth;
when He was reviled,
He did not revile in return;
when He was suffering,
He did not threaten
but entrusted Himself to the One who judges justly.
He Himself bore our sins
in His body on the tree,
so that, having died to sins,
we might live for righteousness;
you have been healed by His wounds.
For you were like sheep going astray,
but you have now returned
to the Shepherd and Guardian of your souls.

The cross represents an awesome price paid for you and for me. In this day of religious diversity and sensitivity, we must be careful not to minimize this reality. Some would say there are many ways to God. Though they may not realize it, they are saying Jesus did not have to die. That religious stance grossly distorts the significance of the cross and discounts the price only Jesus could pay. As we read the account, let us remember the awesome price He paid.

Finally, notice *the love He displayed*. In Romans 5:8, we are reminded how "God demonstrates His own love for us in this: While we were still sinners, Christ died for us." In his masterful study of the cross, John Stott wrote:

> The symbol of the religion of Jesus is the cross, not the scales. It is the place ultimate love and complete humility met. Only one act of pure love, untainted by ulterior motive, has ever been performed in history. That is why, if we are looking for a definition of love, we should not look in a dictionary, but at Calvary.[1]

The cross is the clearest example of God's love for us. I hope that these basic, simple truths will serve as the lens through which the cross is magnified in our understanding and our living.

Take a moment to read Luke 22:66-23:56. You will find *The Events of the Day* (Luke 22:66–23:32) and *The Event of Eternity—The Crucifixion of Christ* (Luke 23:33-49).

The Events of the Day

The Trials

The events of the day revolved around the plot to kill Jesus, set in motion earlier in the week and involving Judas' betrayal. Though the religious leaders who engineered the plan had the authority to arrest Jesus, they did not have the authority to kill Him. Their plot had to be played out in the complicated political landscape of Judea. This explains the various trials Jesus endured, as well as the mockery and physical abuse that came in each of the settings. The following is an outline of the four trials recorded by Luke:

Trial By the Sanhedrin (Luke 22:63-71)
Trial Before Pilate (Luke 23:1-5)
Trial Before Herod Antipas (Luke 23:6-12)
Second Trial Before Pilate (Luke 23:13-25)

A CLOSER LOOK

Understanding the Power Structures in Jerusalem

ILLUSTRATOR PHOTO/ BOB SCHATZ (10/28/6)

D ifficult political dynamics surrounded the trials of Jesus. The Jewish people deeply resented the Romans who were ruling the nation at that time, but the Romans were far superior in their military might. The Roman governor of Judea was Pontius Pilate. Pilate and the Jews equally disdained each other. Though the Romans held control, they also attempted to appease the conquered Jewish people by recognizing and empowering certain religious and political leaders. The religious leadership the Romans recognized was the Sanhedrin, the ruling body for the temple and the representatives of the people in Jerusalem.

The local political leadership was complicated as well. Different leaders had jurisdiction over different regions of Judea. Herod Antipas, the son of Herod the Great, was the recognized and authorized political leader of Galilee, the region from which Jesus came. Herod happened to be in Jerusalem during the time of the Passover. Each of these ruling entities had a deep distrust of one another and they were constantly trying to undermine one another.

Above: Inscription found at Caesarea Maritima mentioning Pontius Pilate and Tiberias, the governor

Lower left: The steps Jesus was led up to Caiphus's house next to the Church of St. Peter's in Gallicantu

After being found guilty by the Sanhedrin, Jesus was taken to Pontius Pilate. Pilate could find no fault in Jesus and would have released Him if not for the insistence of the religious leaders. Instead, He sent Jesus to Herod Antipas, a reprobate leader of the worst kind. Herod made sport of Jesus, asking Him to perform a miracle for Him. When Jesus did not cooperate or even answer, Herod lost interest and sent Him back to Pilate. Ironically, until that time, Pilate and Herod did not get along. Luke records, "That very day Herod and Pilate became friends. Previously, they had been hostile toward each other" (23:12).

While a new friendship was beginning, the conflict was not resolved. Once again Pilate was faced with the decision of what to do with Jesus. Rather than killing Him, Pilate proposed the middle ground of a flogging. This did not appease the religious leaders. Instead, they appealed to a Roman custom, which occurred at Passover, of setting free a prisoner of the people's choice. Pilate desired to release Jesus, but the religious leaders and the crowd that was heavily influenced by them chose a man named Barrabas (23:18). When Pilate asked the crowds what he should do with Jesus, for the first time we hear the chilling words, "Crucify! Crucify Him!" (23:20). Luke

ILLUSTRATOR PHOTO/ BRENT BRUCE (60/0639)

23:25 records that Pilate "handed Jesus over to their will." Sadly, Jesus was sentenced to die for being exactly who He was, the King of the Jews.

The Journey to the Cross (Luke 23:26-31)

Luke does not go into detail about the events between Jesus' trial and the journey to the cross. The other Gospels tell us about the vicious flogging, the hateful taunting of the soldiers, the mockery of a royal robe, and the cruel crown of thorns thrust onto His head. Instead, Luke simply recounts the facts of the journey. His Gospel tells of Simon the Cyrenian who shared in the suffering of our Lord and became a living symbol of what Jesus had previously taught that His followers must do (Luke 9:23; 14:27). Simon would both carry the cross and follow the Savior.

As Jesus walked the path of shame and suffering, Luke recounts there was a great crowd following Him. No doubt many followed simply as curious onlookers, others as hateful scoffers. But Luke records there were women who followed, mourning and lamenting Him. Amazingly, in the midst of His personal anguish and pain, Jesus comforted them (23:28-31). One final detail Luke records about the road to the cross is

ILLUSTRATOR PHOTO/ BOB SCHATZ (35/43/12)

that there were two criminals who were "led away to be executed with Him" (23:32). While all of the Gospel writers include that Jesus was crucified between two criminals, it is only Luke who recorded the conversation that ensued. In Luke's remembrance, these two men were a major part of the story. The stage is now set for the most staggering event in all of eternity.

The Event of Eternity: The Cross of Jesus Christ

With striking simplicity, Luke records the moment with this succinct statement, "When they arrived at the place called the Skull, they crucified Him there" (Luke 23:33). This moment was the central event of all time and eternity. The cross is the focal point of history and the source of our salvation. In his powerful book, *Experiencing the Cross*, Henry Blackaby carefully described this moment in the context of the heart and mind of God, saying:

> When we speak of the cross in its larger biblical meaning, we aren't thinking just of the crucifixion of Jesus.... It's a much bigger picture than that. In fact, we're viewing God's entire plan to redeem the world. We're looking at the whole redemptive event ... as God sees it, not just as we perceive it.... To fully understand it, we must

see the cross as the whole work of God that began in eternity.... Just as the shadow of the cross reaches back into eternity, so it also thrusts forward. The full meaning of the cross ultimately includes the resurrection of Jesus.[2]

Indeed, the cross not only reaches forward to the moment of resurrection, but also reaches forward to us today. The ramifications of this moment are hard to comprehend. Yet, though the cross transcends time, it is important to remember that it happened in time. Luke's account will give us the unique viewpoint of a dialogue between Jesus and the two criminals crucified on His right and left. Before we stand at the foot of the cross and observe this moment, let us step back and take a closer look at the reality of Luke's understated words, "they crucified Him there."

A CLOSER LOOK
Crucifixion

Crucifixion was a horrific punishment. An invention of the Persians somewhere in the third century B.C., it was adopted as an instrument of punishment by the Romans. Though the Romans did not invent crucifixion, they employed its use more than any other group and perfected it as a cruel instrument of death. The practice often involved flogging beforehand and the public spectacle of the accused carrying the crossbar to the place of crucifixion, often a designated, public place. Upon arrival, the victim was stripped to a simple loincloth, or completely naked, and was nailed to the crossbar with arms outstretched. Following this, the victim would be raised up, affixed to the cross with legs slightly bent, and would be nailed to the upright beam of the cross at their ankles. A small block or plank of wood jutted out from the upright beam as a sort of uncomfortable seat that prolonged the agony of death by supporting some of the weight. This was only the beginning. The hours to come would lead to the excruciating pain from the nails driven through the wrists and ankles. As agonizing fatigue set in, breathing became labored leading to a slow asphyxiation.

Cicero, a Roman statesman who lived in the first century, spoke against crucifixion saying it was, "a most cruel and disgusting penalty." Though the act of crucifixion was gruesome, the entire experience was designed to be a deterrent to other potential evildoers.

Left: The twelfth station of the cross on the Via Dolorosa is in Church of the Holy Sepulcher. This interior of the church shows the altar which marks the location of the cross.

Josephus, the first century historian, gives us an eye witness account of a moment at the fall of Jerusalem in 70 A.D., when the conquering Romans, led by Titus, used crucifixion to extinguish the possibility of future Jewish revolt. Though this event occurred after the crucifixion of Christ, it is a striking description of the cruelty of crucifixion:

> They were first whipped and then tormented with all sorts of tortures

before they died, and were then crucified before the wall of the city. This miserable procedure made Titus greatly to pity them, while they caught every day five hundred Jews; nay, some days they caught more…. The main reason why he did not forbid that cruelty was this, that he hoped the Jews might perhaps yield at that sight, out of fear lest they might themselves afterwards be liable to the same cruel treatment. So the soldiers, out of the wrath and hatred they bore the Jews, nailed those they caught, one after one way, and another after another, to the crosses, by way of jest, when their multitude was so great, that room was wanting for the crosses, and crosses wanting for the bodies.[3]

In his masterful work, *The Cross of Christ*, John Stott described the prolonged agony of crucifixion:

It is probably the most cruel method of execution ever practiced, for it deliberately delayed death until maximum torture had been inflicted. The victim could suffer for days before dying. When the Romans adopted it, they reserved it for criminals convicted of murder, rebellion or armed robbery, provided that they were also slaves, foreigners or other non-persons.[4]

Indeed, this "non-person" was the One who was fully God, fully man, and completely faithful to fulfill God's chosen purpose. For roughly six hours on that Friday, Jesus would experience the horrors of a terrible death. It was publicly shameful, intensely painful, and excruciatingly fatal. What Luke described in only a few words, "they crucified Him there," brings us face to face with the reality of all that our Savior would endure on our behalf that day.

The Cross, The Criminals, and The Crucified Christ (Luke 23:32-47)

At the place called The Skull, Jesus was crucified along with the two criminals, one on the right and one on the left. It is here Luke records the amazing words of Jesus, "Father, forgive them, because they do not know what they are doing" (23:34). Unmoved by these grace-filled words, the soldiers callously gambled for His clothes at the foot of the cross.

Luke alone recorded the ensuing conversation between the criminals crucified on each side of Jesus (23:39-43). These three men who likely had no interaction with one another prior to this moment, now faced the end of their lives together. Years ago, I heard a message about the cross. I don't remember the preacher's name, but I remember the points he made. He said that when someone was on the cross he could only look forward, he could make no future plans, and he was certain that he would soon die. All three points are accurate truths. However, in the case of the two criminals, the middle truth could be changed because of the man in the middle.

I have often thought about how Jesus was strategically placed between these two unnamed men whose eternity hung in the balance as they hung on their crosses. They were given equal access to Jesus, but had very different reactions to Him. As they were nailed to their respective crosses they would hear the cries from Jesus, not cursing those who nailed His hands to the cross, but asking for the Father's forgiveness. Even as Jesus' hands reached out to them both, their responses revealed the condition of their hearts. Their individual decisions capture the two dramatically different responses we can make as we stand at the foot of the cross.

The response of the first criminal was absolute rejection of Jesus. As the crowds watched, the religious leaders and the soldiers continually mocked Jesus, saying, "He saved others; let Him save Himself if this is God's Messiah, the Chosen One!" Surprisingly one of the criminals began to join the chorus of criticism, repeating the words that he was hearing, "Aren't You the Messiah? Save Yourself and us!" (23:39). These words were not genuine words of faith; they were sneering accusations of unbelief. This criminal absolutely rejected the Christ. Perhaps the greatest tragedy of this Friday was the faithless response of this criminal who would enter eternity without Christ and without hope. Unfortunately, there are those who stand two thousand years later and make the same decision to absolutely reject the love, forgiveness, and hope offered by Jesus.

The other criminal quickly responded, rebuking his hardhearted friend, "Don't you even fear God, since you are undergoing the same punishment? We are punished justly, because we're getting back what we deserve for the things we did, but this man has done nothing wrong" (23:40-41). Then he turned to Jesus and said, "Jesus, remember me when You come into Your kingdom!" (23:42). While the first prisoner rejected Jesus, notice that this one demonstrated astounding faith. As he looked to Jesus, he looked into the eyes of a dying man. He fixed his eyes on the bloody and mangled man that had been beaten, bruised, slashed, gashed, and nailed to the cross. This criminal had no real evidence that Jesus would reign over a coming, eternal kingdom. Yet he believed. He did not have the benefit of knowing the rest of the story, that in three days time this dying Savior would become the resurrected Lord. Yet he believed! He chose in the moment of his death to believe that the One on the cross beside him was the very Author of life. His was an astounding faith. When we believe, our faith may astound those who do not understand or choose not to believe. This criminal's faith reminds us that the circumstances are never too dark and the time is never too late to trust the Savior.

These two criminals remind us the cross was not just an event in history; it is a timeless invitation to all people.

These two criminals remind us the cross was not just an event in history; it is a timeless invitation to all people. This invitation demands a response, but allows for individual decision. What is your response to Jesus?

While you think about that question, don't fail to see Jesus' response. Jesus answered with these beautiful words, "I assure you: Today you will be with Me in paradise." Luke tells us it was about noon and with these words darkness came over the whole land until three. At three, the curtain of the temple, the one dividing the holy of holies from the holy place and all of the outer courts, was split down the middle (23:44-45). No longer would sinful man lack access to a holy heavenly Father. Then, Jesus cried out in a loud voice, "Father, into your hands I entrust My spirit." Having said this Jesus breathed His last.

Jesus' response to the criminal and the events that followed show us the decision that is most important. Amazingly, Jesus had chosen to offer His unmerited love, even to those He knew would reject Him. The torn curtain in the temple dramatically demonstrated what Jesus had promised the faith-filled felon: no one is beyond the amazing grace of our loving Lord. By His grace, a guilty criminal would become a pardoned participant that very day in the kingdom of God. And now, we too, by faith can enter His grace and experience the fullness of His presence and live in the hope of His promise. His decision has been made, has yours?

As Jesus breathed His last breath, experiencing the sweet relief of a completed mission, Luke records that the centurion began to glorify God. This man was probably responsible for the overseeing of the entire crucifixion. He would have observed every moment of this central event of all eternity. His response? "This man really was righteous!" (23:47). I'm not exactly certain what this soldier's response meant, but I think this moment of spontaneous praise and the declaration of Jesus' righteousness was evidence of what we celebrate on this, the worst good day of history. This Jesus of Nazareth, the King of the Jews, was the crucified Christ.

Our journey is not yet complete, but we have now seen Jesus walk the hardest part of the path. I pray we have seen the cross clearly. If we were standing at the foot of the cross on that day in the moments that followed, we would observe Jesus' broken, lifeless body removed from the cross and prepared for burial by broken-hearted followers (23:50-56). Before they come, let us stand at the foot of the cross and join the centurion by glorifying God. There are so many songs that have been birthed out of the inspiration of this central event of eternity, but let us borrow the words of the great hymn writer, Isaac Watts, to give voice to our praise. May these words be the desire of our hearts and the decision that guides our lives.

When I Survey the Wondrous Cross

When I survey the wondrous cross
On which the Prince of Glory died;
My richest gain I count but loss,
And pour contempt on all my pride.

Forbid it, Lord, that I should boast,
Save in the death of Christ, my God!
All the vain things that charm me most,
I sacrifice them to His blood.

See, from His head, His hands, His feet,
Sorrow and love flow mingled down.

Did e'er such love and sorrow meet,
Or thorns compose so rich a crown?

Were the whole realm of nature mine,
That were a present far too small;
Love so amazing, so divine,
Demands my soul, my life, my all.

Questions for the Journey

1. What is your earliest recollection of the cross?

2. How is your life different because of what took place on Good Friday?

3. How do the events of that Friday make you feel?

4. Can you identify with both of the criminals on the cross? Why or why not?

5. What do you think the centurion's confession meant to him?

6. What is your favorite song about the cross?

7. Thinking of all that Christ sacrificed (Himself, His position, His authority, His comfort) for the glory of God, what are you prepared to sacrifice to focus more completely on Christ and His purposes in the world?

8. Have you noticed the cross being used as jewelry or decorations? Consider committing yourself to using the cross in these settings as a discussion starter focused on a person's relationship with Christ.

Thank You for the Cross

Write a letter to Christ, thanking Him for making the worst day in history the best day for you, and explaining why this is so.

1. John Stott, *The Cross of Christ* (Downers Grove, IL: InterVarsity Press, 1986) 212.
2. Henry Blackaby, *Experiencing the Cross: Your Greatest Opportunity for Victory Over Sin* (Colorado Springs, CO: Multnomah Books, 2005) 9-10.
3. Josephus, *Wars of the Jews*. 5.11.1.
4. John Stott, 29.

CHAPTER SIX

SATURDAY

Resting in the Reality of the Empty Cross

LUKE 23:50-56

And they rested on the Sabbath according to the commandment
(Luke 23:56).

There was very little time to process the events of the week. They blurred together like a terrible tapestry that was a horrible reality. The details were still sketchy, but it was clear that a tragedy had occurred. The One in whom the disciples had placed their hopes was now dead. Luke 23:49 records the events of the last moments of that Friday, "But all who knew Him, including the women who had followed Him from Galilee, stood at a distance, watching these things." Death brought such disturbing distance. Yet, there was no time to mourn. It was just hours from the Sabbath, and there was work to be done. Jesus' body had to be removed from the cross. His followers could not bear the thought of simply leaving Him there. Surely, they had seen it before—victims' bodies left on the cross for days as the scavenging birds gathered. No, that would not be the case for Jesus. Somehow, someway, they would remove His body for a proper burial.

There were so many questions. Could they get permission to remove His body? If so, where would they bury Him? Would they have time to properly prepare the body? What had just happened and why? What now? There was no time to process all the thoughts that must have rushed through their minds. It was late on Friday afternoon, the day of preparation for the Sabbath (Luke 23:54). The Sabbath day would officially begin just after sunset and all work would have to cease.

News came that Joseph of Arimathea, a wealthy member of the Sanhedrin, was providing a tomb for Jesus' burial. Even more than that, he secured permission from Pilate to remove Jesus' body. Interestingly, Joseph disagreed with the decisions of the Sanhedrin and was speaking as if he believed in the coming kingdom of which Jesus had spoken. Having removed Jesus' body, they hurriedly prepared it for burial. There was not time to wrap the body with the customary spices and perfumes. That would have to come later, perhaps on Sunday. For now, a simple linen shroud would be wrapped

around His body and the tomb would be sealed with a stone. With the setting of the sun, it was the Sabbath.

Luke records only the brief words, "And they rested on the Sabbath according to the commandment" (23:56). Some have called this day Silent Saturday. The silence refers to the lack of information the Gospel writers provide. There was no teaching to report. There were no miracles mentioned. It was a day when God seemed silent.

Only Matthew breaks the silence regarding the day, recording that the Pharisees requested Pilate to deploy soldiers to seal and guard the tomb. It seems on this day the

Pharisees had greater clarity about Jesus' teaching than His disciples. They remembered Jesus had said, "After three days, I will rise again" (Matt. 27:63). Their concern was that "the last deception will be worse than the first" (Matt. 27:63-64). Pilate granted their requests, thwarting any attempts of Jesus' disciples to steal His body. They "made the tomb secure by sealing the stone and setting the guard" (Matt. 27:66). It was not a completely silent day, but the only sounds were those that sealed the despair that filled the silence. It would not remain that way long, but the silence must have been deafening.

Jesus followers were living in a unique place between future promise and present fulfillment, between faith and sight. This was the moment when the cross was empty, but the grave was filled. They were living in the angst of the unresolved promise. Everyone who follows Jesus will experience those "in-between moments," where we live in the silent place between the promise and the realization. It is actually a place of perceived silence. God has spoken and now is in the process of bringing about what He promised. In truth, these moments serve a purpose in the process of fulfillment. Jesus had prepared those closest to Him for this moment. He told them He would be in the grave for three days. Now, they had to believe the promise and wait for the time of fulfillment. Their faith was challenged. In similar ways, we are all faced with the decision to trust God's promises, or to struggle in personal anxiety. While it may be a place of current incompletion, it is not a place where the outcome is uncertain. He has promised; and He will fulfill. The waiting period is the difficult place of silence.

On this day of relative silence, God provided an opportunity for the disciples to rest. The word *rest* often is foreign to us. It seems so … well, unproductive. "They rested on the Sabbath according to the commandment."

Left: Ramathaim, the home of Joseph of Arimathea

Below: Artist rendition of a Roman legionnaire

To be specific, the fourth commandment states, "You are to labor six days and do all your work, but the seventh day is a Sabbath to the Lord your God. You must not do any work.... For the Lord made the heavens and the earth, the sea, and everything in them in six days; then He rested on the seventh day. Therefore the Lord blessed the Sabbath day and declared it holy" (Ex. 20:9-11). How difficult it must have been to rest on that day. Finally, after the frantic events of Friday, they were alone with their thoughts. They must have been exhausted by the events of the week. I wonder if they thought of Jesus' words, "Come to Me, all of you who are weary and burdened, and I will give you rest" (Matt. 11:28). What about now? How could they rest in Him now? It must have been a difficult day for them. Though they did not realize it then, the blood-stained, empty cross bore testimony that there was a new reality in which to rest.

On the seventh day of the first week in history, God, having completed the work of creation, rested. Now, on the seventh day of the greatest week in history, Jesus, having completed the work of redemption, rested. This will be the most unique day of our journey because the One we've been following, and will follow again, is silent in His rest. On this day of rest, I invite you to reflect on and rest in the silent testimony of an empty cross.

LEARNING ACTIVITY

Hardest Part of Waiting

You are planting this seed. What are some of the stages the seed will go through in order to produce vegetables?

Questions for Reflection

1. Has God ever seemed silent when you felt you needed to hear from Him?

2. What did you learn about God and yourself during that silence?

3. What do you need to rearrange in order to have a regular day of rest?

4. How have the "in-between times" strengthened your faith?

Left: The Garden Tomb at Jerusalem, which dates to the 2nd or 3rd centuries AD, is situated near Gordon's Calvary, a hillock just outside Damascus gate at Jerusalem. A British scholar named Gordon in the last century felt evidence was strong indicating these sites as the actual sites of Christ's death, burial and resurrection, instead of the ones now beneath the Church of the Holy Sepulchre. Most scholars still believe that the Church of the Holy Sepulchre marks the actual site which is based on a very early tradition.

The Empty Cross and the Finished Work of Jesus Christ

The empty cross is a powerful symbol of the finished work of Christ at the cross. "It is finished," was the cry of Jesus recorded by John in his Gospel account of Jesus' death (19:30). Those three powerful words summarize the reality of the empty cross. Jesus' work was completed.

I stumbled on a strong truth almost by accident when I served as pastor of Edgewater Baptist Church in New Orleans. One Sunday after a worship service, a young man approached me. He explained that this was his first time at our church or any Baptist church. He was very complimentary, and then shared that he had a question. He had been raised as a Roman Catholic and was accustomed to seeing crucifixes, crosses with the likeness of Christ suffering on the cross. He explained that the crucifix was a powerful symbol of his beliefs. In his weekly worship experience, the crucifix helped him focus on the sacrifice Jesus made for him. I wasn't sure where he was going with this information, but I kept listening. Then he asked the question, "Why is your cross empty?" It was a good question. I had never really thought about it. I stalled for time saying, "That is a really interesting question, and I'm not sure I know the right answer." Then, I shared the first thought that came to my mind, "I guess our cross is empty because He is not there anymore." Since then I have thought about that question many times as I have seen crucifixes and "empty" crosses in many settings throughout the world. I'm sure there are better answers, but I don't think I would go back and change my answer. We both grew in our understanding of the Lord from our conversation, but I walked away with a new awareness. Though we remember the sacrifice Jesus made on the cross, He is not there anymore. The empty cross reminds us that Jesus finished His work on the cross. On that Saturday, He rested in that completed work.

I have come to realize that the reality of the empty cross has a theological description. It is often called the finished work of Christ. This reality has inspired millions of people to share their own personal reflections, expressing their thoughts through poetry and prose, paintings and sculptures, sermons and songs. We have at our disposal so many God-given resources to aid us in our moments of wrestling. Most notably, this theme becomes the focal point of the gospel message as the writers of the New Testament explained it. Inspired by the Holy Spirit, they reflected on the reality of the cross and explained it theologically. As we reflect on the empty cross, I would like to offer three truths in which we can rest.

1. Sacrifice has been made—He has done what had to be done.
The first and most striking truth is that Jesus became the sacrifice for our sins. Having lived a sinless life, He died an atoning death. The New Testament writers began to realize that Christ's death was the fulfillment of the sacrificial images from the Old Testament, most notably the Passover sacrifice and the Day of Atonement sacrifice (Lev. 16; 23:27-28). We have discussed the Passover sacrifice at length (see Thursday in this study). The writer of Hebrews summarized the annual Day of Atonement sacrifice: "But in the sacrifice, there is a reminder of sins every year. For it is impossible for the blood of bulls and goats to take away sins" (Heb. 10:3-4). This explanation was followed by the profound explanation of how Jesus' death on the cross was the once and for all sacrifice:

Left: Gordon's Calvary was proposed in the 1800s by a British man named Gordon to be the site of Jesus' crucifixion. Because caves on its cliff face form skull-like eye sockets and its close proximity to an ancient tomb, Gordon's theory was taken seriously by scholars. However, further evidence indicates the tomb nearby actually dates to the 2nd or 3rd centuries.

By this will of God, we have been sanctified through the offering of the body of Jesus Christ once and for all. Every priest stands day after day ministering and offering the same sacrifices time after time, which can never take away sins. But this man, after offering one sacrifice for sins forever, sat down at the right hand of God. He is now waiting until His enemies are made His footstool. For by one offering He has perfected forever those who are sanctified (Heb. 10:10-14).

Jesus did what had to be done, and what only He could do. We can rest in the reality of this Savior. This leads me to the second truth.

2. Sins can be forgiven—He can do what needs to be done.

The empty cross stands as a constant reminder that our sins can be forgiven. By embracing the sacrifice Jesus made on the cross, we can experience personal forgiveness for our sins. By faith, we must embrace the finished work of Christ on the cross. In so doing, we can experience the life-changing forgiveness of Jesus Christ.

At the cross, Jesus dealt with the darkness of our sin. He looked clearly at the moments in your life you are most ashamed of, and every other moment of failure in your life, and He chose to forgive. The empty cross reminds me I can rest in the fact that Jesus was willing to die for the darkest of my sins. Have you ever really stopped to think about that? When Jesus died on the cross, He was not dying for your best efforts or your greatest accomplishments. The darkness of our hearts becomes the backdrop that displays the depths of His love. Paul expressed this powerfully in Romans 3:21-26:

> But now, apart from the law, God's righteousness has been revealed—attested by the Law and the Prophets—that is, God's righteousness through faith in Jesus Christ, to all who believe, since there is no distinction. For all have sinned and fall short of the glory of God. They are justified freely by His grace through the redemption that is in Christ Jesus. God presented Him as a propitiation through faith in His blood, to demonstrate His righteousness, because in His restraint God passed over the sins previously committed. God presented Him to demonstrate His righteousness at the present time, so that He would be righteous and declare righteous the one who has faith in Jesus.

Rest in the reality that the empty cross means your sins can be forgiven. For some, that will mean for the very first time you will trust Christ to forgive you and to give you a brand new start. If you have never experienced His forgiveness in your life, you can call on Him in prayer. He will hear and answer your prayer. He will become your personal Savior and Lord.

**Rest in the reality that the empty cross means
your sins can be forgiven.**

For others, you know Jesus Christ as Savior and Lord, but you are not living in the reality of the freedom of forgiveness. Perhaps you are struggling with receiving the Lord's forgiveness for something that happened in your life years ago. Maybe, you are struggling with offering forgiveness to someone who has wronged you. Maybe, the depth of your personal sins has left deep wounds. Though you know you are forgiven, you need to invite the Lord to not only forgive, but also to help you begin a process of healing.

It might be that the depth and intensity of a season of rebellion has taken you far away from the presence of the Lord. You even wonder if He can forgive you for what you have done. He can. He will. But you must believe it, ask for it, and receive it.

3. You don't have to fear the future—He will do what He has promised.

Finally, the empty cross reminds us we don't have to fear the future. The empty cross is the powerful promise that there will also be an empty tomb. Historically, we see that what God has promised, He soon delivers. Tomorrow, we will celebrate the greatest day in history, the day when the promises of our crucified Savior are fulfilled by the living example of our risen Lord. We do not have to fear. I have heard it said that the single most repeated command of Jesus was, "Do not be afraid." Why? Because He has done what needed to be done, and He will do all that has been promised by the Father. This is especially true during those heart-wrenching moments of life when we feel He is least aware of, or involved in, the challenges of our lives. When we lose sight of His working, we can always fix our gaze on the empty cross as a tangible example of faithfulness. I love the often-quoted words of Corrie ten Boom, "There is no pit so deep that His love is not deeper still." [1]

"There is no pit so deep that His love is not deeper still."
– Corrie ten Boom

One of my favorite passages that illustrate this truth is in Romans 8. This chapter is filled with powerful truths, but here are the two verses I have in mind: "What then are we to say about these things? If God is for us, who is against us? He did not even spare His own Son, but offered Him up for us all; how will He not also with Him grant us everything?" (Rom. 8:31-32). Today, rest in the reality of the empty cross.

Questions for Reflection
1. Are there areas of your life where you are struggling to trust God? What are they? Why are you struggling with them?

2. Thinking about the empty cross, how has God spoken in His Word regarding your situation?

3. What promises of God apply directly to your situation?

4. Are there areas of your life where you need to rest in His promise as you await the future fulfillment?

5. How can you trust God in a more tangible way this week?

6. Whom can you ask to pray for you as you learn to trust God more this week?

Promised Truth Becomes Personal Truth

Before we leave this day of rest, I want to encourage you to make sure you allow the promised truth of God to become the personal truth experienced by you. I am always amazed at the ways God takes His general truth and makes it specific to our life circumstances. I am grateful for the many ways, and many times, God has done this in my life. I will close this chapter with a personal story of one of those moments.

I have already introduced you to my wife and kids. Aside from my love for God, they are the greatest loves in my life. They bless my life beyond measure, and I absolutely love the moments we spend together. Our family's schedule is a lot like others in that we don't always have a great deal of time to simply be together. So, when our friends Al and Tracie Denson invited us to spend spring break at their ranch in Texas, we jumped at the opportunity. It had been a particularly draining time for me personally and spiritually, and I couldn't wait to have some time to relax with my family and to have some moments alone with the Lord. We packed our stuff, and I packed my Bible and a blank notebook, and headed out.

The ranch is a beautiful place, located on the rolling hills of East Texas. More than a ranch, it is often a place of retreat. There are amazing cabins, a beautiful chapel where we had opportunities to worship with some close friends, and beautiful scenic vistas in every direction. On top of that, there were ATV's to ride and miles of trails to explore. My kids love the outdoors and adventure, so they were in heaven. We had a blast!

Then it happened. My daughter Rivers came around a corner, and it was apparent she had become a victim of one of the big mud holes that surrounded one of the ponds on the property. She was splattered with mud from head to toe! When I asked what happened (as if it wasn't apparent!), with a big grin on her face she said, "Trea and Ridge got me good!"

Well, after that it was on! Rivers and I decided we would get those "good-for-nothing" boys back. My wife, recognizing this was not going to be a pretty outcome, decided to stay at a safe distance. Revenge did not come easily. In fact, in my attempts to "spray" the boys with mud, I became a sitting duck stuck in the mud. My ruthless boys jumped at the opportunity to take advantage of me. Over and over again, they rode by me and with perfect precision poured streams of mud on top of their helpless dad! It was unbelievable.

Unable to get my four-wheeler free from the mud, I finally decided I would wait until they came around the corner again, and I would pull them off their mud-slinging machines and throw them in the lake. I executed my plan perfectly, and within seconds we were in the chilly waters of a muddy lake, all caked in and covered by mud! By this point, my wife was laughing hard at the mud-covered sight before her eyes. I invited her to join us, but she politely declined to take advantage of the free mud bath she could enjoy for much less than one of those expensive spas. We were a muddy mess!

I decided I would head back to clean up. The boys wanted to keep riding, so I headed back by myself. When I arrived at our cabin, I tried to figure out how to clean up. I

had mud all over my body from head to toe, including in my ears, nose, and mouth. The fun was now over. I grabbed a water hose and attempted to wash off the layers upon layers of clingy mud. With effort, it started coming off, but I knew I was far from clean. Then, I tried to wash it out of my white shirt. Over and over, I would rinse it and wring out the dirty water. I didn't think I would ever be clean again.

COURTESY OF THE WRITER

Above: The cross on the hill at the ranch

Left: The writer after his dip in the muddy lake

That's when it hit me. The Lord spoke gently to my heart. He was the only one who could truly clean me up. By the cross, He had done this and continually cleansed my shortcomings. By His cross, I was blessed to share in His abundant life. As I kept washing, the Lord reminded me of the cross that was placed at the highest point on the ranch. I had seen it just moments before the massacre of mud. On top of that hill was a cross.

I had recognized the physical beauty of the cross on a previous day. Now, covered in mud and mire, the Lord took me again to see the spiritual beauty of the cross. I was overcome with thankfulness and overwhelmed by His love. In that moment, I rested in the reality of the empty cross. His promised truth had once again become personal to me. With a scrub brush and water hose in hand, I started to sing an old hymn our host, Al, had led us in the evening before. It was my prayer then, and is my prayer for you now.

Jesus, keep me near the cross,
There a precious fountain,
Free to all, a healing stream,
Flows from Calvary's mountain.

In the cross, in the cross,
Be my glory ever,
Till my raptured soul shall find
Rest beyond the river.

May we rest this day and every day in the reality of the empty cross.

Scales of Rest

On the left side, above the scale, list the items that cause you to worry. On the right side list above the scale, the things that bring you rest. Which way is your scale weighted? What does this mean?

© 2011 JupiterImages Corporation

1. Corrie Ten Boom, J. Sherril and S. Sherril, *The Hiding Place* (New York: Bantam, 1971), 217.

CHAPTER SEVEN

RESURRECTION SUNDAY

The Greatest Day in History

LUKE 24

On the first day of the week, very early in the morning, they came to the tomb, bringing the spices they had prepared. They found the stone rolled away from the tomb. They went in, but did not find the body of the Lord Jesus. While they were perplexed about this, suddenly two men stood by them in dazzling clothes. So the women were terrified and bowed down to the ground. "Why are you looking for the living among the dead?" asked the men. "He is not here, but He has been resurrected!"
(Luke 24:1-6)

Same Story

Several years ago, our church had an Easter egg hunt on Palm Sunday. After our morning worship service, we gathered at a campground nearby for lunch. Following a great time of fellowship, all of the kids were gathered for the big egg hunt. There were hundreds of kids finding eggs, all of which contained "modern-day manna," also known as chocolate! Having sufficiently filled each child well past his or her sugar quotient, it was now time for me to bring spiritual application to the experience. Gathered by a beautiful lake and armed with a secret weapon called Resurrection Eggs, I embraced my task with courage and confidence. Actually, I prayed God would help me get through it!

As we quieted the kids to a dull roar, I took the Resurrection Eggs out so each of the children could see them. For those unfamiliar with these unique teaching tools, simply imagine a foam egg crate filled with different-colored, plastic eggs. Each of the eggs contained different items representing aspects of the Easter story. I would open each of the eggs to reveal the contents, and then ask the children to help me remember why that symbol was important. There was a small palm branch, a piece of bread, a silver coin, a piece of purple cloth, a small crown of thorns, a nail, a cross, and a rock.

The climax of the story came as I opened the last egg—the empty egg representing the empty tomb. In the last two minutes we talked about that empty tomb and the difference the first Easter made.

Amazingly, the children were captivated by my story-telling abilities. Well, okay, they were actually captivated by the eggs and the symbols they contained. Nonetheless, we walked the same journey in about 10 minutes you and I have walked over the last week. All were captivated, except one little boy. I noticed him out of the corner of my eye. He was one of the older children and was very smart. I noticed him walk back into the crowd of parents gathered behind the children and begin talking to his mom and dad. After he spoke to them, they both laughed and I knew I had to find out what this little guy had said.

I led in a closing prayer asking God to help us celebrate the real meaning of Easter, and then everyone began to leave. The little boy's parents approached me with smiles on their faces. I knew I wouldn't have to ask what he shared with them. They couldn't wait to tell me! The mom explained that the little boy asked if they could leave. When she responded that Pastor Rob wasn't finished yet, the boy replied, "Mom, he's telling the same story he told last year!"

I often think about that little boy when I read the story of that first Easter. Every year we gather to celebrate the same story; it never changes. Yet, within this story is the great reality that though the story never changes, Easter changed everything!

Easter: The Story that Changes Everything!

Left: Interior of the Garden Tomb

Easter is the celebration of the resurrection of Jesus from the dead and the change this reality brings. The resurrection of Jesus Christ is at the very core of all we believe as Christians. John Stott rightly said, "Christianity is in its essence a resurrection religion. The concept of religion lies at its heart. If you remove it, Christianity is destroyed."[1]

Apart from the resurrection, the story of Jesus' amazing life and brutal death might be reduced to a tragedy of the worst kind. The story line might have read something like this: A well-meaning but misguided man died a senseless death, and was placed in a tomb, disproving his claims that he would rise again from the dead. The result would have been devastating to all those who dared to believe, to follow, and to hope in Him. It is interesting to think about, but completely unnecessary.

That is not how the story ended. Instead, those who left the cross believing it was the end would hours later leave the empty tomb aware that this was the entrance into the next chapter of God's work in the world. At the heart of all that they believed and all that we believe is the resurrection.

The first Easter is a powerful record of the change that occurred in the hearts and lives of those who encountered Jesus. In rapid-fire succession, the story unfolds with each life-changing encounter with the risen Lord. Their story became the basis for the message the early church would proclaim. In a very short time, the story of Easter became the summary of the Gospel. Paul's words to the church at Corinth illustrate that clear message:

> For I passed on to you as most important what I also received: that Christ died for our sins according to the Scriptures, that He was buried, that He was raised on the third day according to the Scriptures, and that He appeared to Cephas, then to the Twelve. Then He appeared to over 500 brothers at one time. ... Then He appeared to James, then to all the apostles (1 Cor. 15:3-7).

Paul's words are like an echo of the angels' voices at the empty tomb when they said, "He is not here, but He has been resurrected!" This message brought together the whole story of the Gospel. The empty tomb proved what the empty cross demonstrated—Jesus is the Savior and the Lord!

As we experience the last day of our journey in the greatest week of history, we find ourselves marveling at this empty tomb. The empty tomb is the powerful symbol demonstrating the change Easter brings. However, the most powerful demonstration is not in the symbol, it is in the presence of the Savior. Bruce Larson said it well, "The events of Easter cannot be reduced to a creed or philosophy. We are not asked to believe the doctrine of the resurrection. We are asked to meet this person raised from the dead. In faith, we move from belief in a doctrine to the knowledge of a person. Ultimate truth is a person. We met Him. He is alive."[2]

Simply put, the living Lord is the greatest evidence that He is the way, the truth, and the life. His resurrection is at the heart of all we believe and proclaim.

LEARNING ACTIVITY

Resurrection Nonsense

Below is a list of theories that try to disprove Christ's resurrection. Check the ones you have heard.

___ The women and the disciples went to the wrong tomb.

___ Jesus never really died on the cross and was revived in the coolness of the night (the swoon theory).

___ The disciples stored the body.

___ Jesus continued to live in some "spiritual" sense that did not involve a bodily resurrection.

___ The disciples were hallucinating.

List additional theories you have heard.

On this greatest day in history we will once again let Luke lead us to experience the empty tomb and the encounters of the day. His account of the first Easter is found in Luke 24. As we walk through this chapter, we will explore the unique change that came from each personal encounter with the risen Lord. In each section below, take a moment to read the account and then consider the change.

The Women (Luke 24:1-11)
Easter Turned Devastation into Celebration

The first group to encounter the reality of the resurrection was a small group of women. Luke did not immediately record all of their names (he will reveal some of their names in Luke 24:10 as Mary Magdalene, Joanna, and Mary, the mother of James), but focused instead on their experience. These women were the ones who had come to the tomb prepared to finish the work of burial. Instead, they became the first people to ever share the good news of His resurrection. Many things could be said about the change that occurred in their lives that day, but it is clear the devastation they were feeling when they came to the tomb quickly turned to celebration as they left. After the angels announced Jesus was resurrected, they reminded the women what Jesus told them some time before back in Galilee: "The Son of Man must be betrayed into the hands of sinful men, be crucified, and rise on the third day." (Luke 24:7). Apparently, they did remember and quickly went to find the 11 disciples to report what they had been told. Can you imagine the excitement in their voices as they tried to convince the disciples of what they had experienced? It was difficult for the disciples to grasp what they were saying. In fact, Luke 24:11 records, "these words seemed like nonsense to them, and they did not believe the women." Though the disciples would join the celebration later, it had begun in the hearts of these ladies. Easter can turn devastation into celebration.

Below: Roman (Eastern Mediterranean) glass vessels in a variety of shapes that indicate the different uses for each piece. These bottles were to hold perfumes, balms, and sacrificial oils.

Simon Peter (Luke 24:12,34; 1 Peter 1:3)
Easter Turned Deep Disappointment into Living Hope

The second encounter involved Simon Peter. Luke's account of Peter's encounter seems somewhat incomplete, but was no less impactful. As the women were celebrating and the disciples were struggling to believe, Luke records, "Peter, however, got up and ran to the tomb. Bending over, he saw the strips of linen lying by themselves, and he went away, wondering to himself what had happened" (Luke 24:12). From there, Luke shifted his focus to yet another encounter that would occur on the road to Emmaus that we will examine in a moment. For now, we jump ahead to the moment when the Emmaus' road disciples reported they had seen the living Lord. They were received by the disciples with much more affirmation than the women had received, probably because of the testimony of Peter. Luke 24:34 notes the response of the eleven to the Emmaus road disciples, "The Lord has certainly been raised, and has appeared to Simon!"

Somewhere between the empty tomb and that moment, Peter encountered the living Lord. Once again, much could be said about this encounter, but I have chosen to focus on the personal impact Jesus made on Peter's life. After the disappointing failure of denying Jesus three times, Peter was broken-hearted and deeply disappointed in himself (22:61-62). While it was probably later along the shores of the Sea of Galilee that Jesus convincingly restored Simon Peter (John 21), in this first encounter Peter was given a glimpse of hope. Later he would write, "Blessed be the God and Father of our Lord Jesus Christ. According to His great mercy, He has given us a new birth into a living hope through the resurrection of Jesus Christ from the dead" (1 Pet. 1:3) Easter can turn deep disappointment into living hope.

The Emmaus Road Disciples (Luke 24:13-35)
Easter Turned Confusion into Conviction

Luke's longest account of an Easter encounter involves two little-known disciples. One was named Cleopas and the other's name was not mentioned. While we are not given many details about these two followers of Christ, we learn a great deal about them from their encounter with Christ.

We know they were going in the wrong direction. While all of the action was occurring in Jerusalem, these disciples were walking away from the city. Luke records they were walking "to a village called Emmaus which was about seven miles from Jerusalem" (24:15). As they traveled, we learn even more about them from their discussion and disposition. Luke says they were discussing and arguing the accounts of the day when Jesus joined them, though they were prevented from recognizing Him. When He asked them about their argument, they looked discouraged. They were amazed that this poor traveler was so out of touch with the events of the last several days and began to explain why their dispositions were so downcast. Listen to their words:

> "The things concerning Jesus the Nazarene, Who was a Prophet powerful in action and speech before God and all the people, and how

Left: Artist's rendition of Peter and John running to the sepulchre of the resurrection; Eugene Burnand, 1898

our chief priests and leaders handed Him over to be sentenced to death, and they crucified Him. But we were hoping that He was the One who was about to redeem Israel. Besides all this, it's the third day since these things happened. Moreover, some women from our group astounded us. They arrived early at the tomb, and they didn't find His body, they came and reported that they had seen a vision of angels who said He was alive. Some of those who were with us went to the tomb and found it just as the women had said, but they didn't see Him" (Luke 24:19-24).

From that moment, Jesus began to turn their confusion into clarity. Through firm yet patient explanation, He walked with them on the road to Emmaus explaining the way of God's redemptive purposes. From Moses to the Prophets, Jesus "interpreted for them the things concerning Himself in all the Scriptures" (Luke 24:27). What an amazing experience that must have been!

As they arrive at their destination, they insisted that their fellow traveler stay with them for a while. As they sat down for a meal, Jesus blessed the meal and broke the bread. At that moment, they knew who He was. Just as quickly as their confusion disappeared, so did Jesus from their presence. His work was done. Their confusion was converted into a burning conviction:

> So they said to each other, "Weren't our hearts burning within us while He was talking with us on the road and explaining the Scriptures to us?" That very hour they got up and returned to Jerusalem. They found the Eleven and those with them gathered together, who said, "The Lord has appeared to Simon!" Then they began to describe what had happened on the road and how He was made known to them in the breaking of the bread (Luke 24:32-35).

There is so much that can be learned from this encounter, yet we will limit our focus to a simple insight: Jesus goes to out of the way places for little-known, or unknown, people so that they can know Him. Easter can turn confusion into conviction.

The Disciples (Luke 24:36-47)
Easter Turned Unbelief into Unshakable Commitment

The last encounter took place as the 11 disciples and those gathered with them were listening to the Emmaus road disciples share their amazing encounter. The moment is described in Luke 24:36-40:

Left: Road and ruins outside the church at El-Qubeibeh, the Franciscan's traditional site of Emmaus. This is one of four possible locations of Emmaus.

And as they were saying these things, He Himself stood among them. He said to them, "Peace to you!" But they were startled and terrified and thought they were seeing a ghost. "Why are you troubled?" He asked them. "And why do doubts arise in your hearts? Look at My hands and My feet, that it is I Myself! Touch Me and see, because a ghost does not have flesh and bones as you can see I have." Having said this He showed them His hands and His feet.

After this stunning moment of show and tell, the disciples were still struggling with believing. Luke records, "they still could not believe because of their joy" (Luke 24:41). Surprisingly, seeing was not enough for believing. They understood what they were seeing, but they did not understand what it meant. They were overjoyed, but were uninformed. This was not the first time they had struggled to understand or to believe, but this time the evidence was overwhelming on so many levels. After eating some broiled fish, Jesus patiently nurtured their fledgling faith

> Then He told them, "These are my words that I spoke to you while I was still with you—that everything written about Me in the Law of Moses, the Prophets, and the Psalms, must be fulfilled." Then he opened their minds to understand the Scriptures. He also said to them, "This is what is written: the Messiah would suffer and rise from the dead the third day, and repentance for forgiveness of sins would be proclaimed in His name to all the nations, beginning at Jerusalem" (Luke 24:44-47).

His words began to sink deeply into their hearts. His completed mission would become their message. Furthermore, sharing this message was now the mission Jesus had given to them. They were now to take this Good News to all nations, to all people! It was beginning to make sense. Their unbelief slowly began to give way to a bold faith that would become an unshakable commitment. Their commitment was not completely evident at this point. Yet, over the course of their lives, each of these disciples demonstrated an unshakable and unaltered commitment to the risen and returning Lord.

While there are many evidences of the resurrection of Jesus, among the greatest is the result of this encounter with the risen Lord. There were undeniable changes that occurred in the lives of Jesus' disciples. They were transformed from a confused, frightened, and defeated group into courageous and emboldened leaders who would sacrifice everything they had, including their lives, to turn the world upside down. Their commitment became the seed of the community of faith that would consist of Jews, Gentiles, slaves, free, male, female, rich, and poor. They broke down every ethnic and cultural barrier because of the fact of the resurrection. They would sacrifice resources, property, reputation, vocations, and positions because they saw and believed. They believed Jesus had changed their lives and could change the world. Yet, it began at this moment of encounter when Jesus met them at their place of unbelief and helped move them to an unshakable commitment. They found the meaning of life in their encounter with the Living One! Easter can turn belief into an unshakable commitment.

Devoted Disciples—Then and Now
Easter Turned Passive Observers Into Powerful Witnesses
(Luke 24:48-49)

One last encounter remains. You will have to look closely in the text to find this final group—and a diverse group they are. Some are full of potential but far from performing. Some are battle-scarred and road-weary, for they have been faithful to follow in the footsteps of their crucified and risen King. Some are confused, some are distracted, and some are decidedly undecided about their own personal commitment. These are the ranks of the devoted disciples of Jesus Christ who dare to follow Him. These are the disciples Jesus loves today and goes out of His way to find. Over two thousand years later, if you look closely in Luke's account, you can see them. In fact, you can see you! Suddenly we find ourselves standing just behind the disciples, listening with them to the resurrected Lord. Jesus' challenge to them is a commission for which we have been recruited! We are not simply observers of all that we have seen, heard, and experienced on our journey of the last week—we have been called to be participants. Can you find your face in the crowd of devoted disciples now gathering around Jesus? Listen closely to His words:

> You are witnesses of these things. And look,
> I am sending you what My Father promised
> (Luke 24:48-49).

Now I recognize that these words were spoken in time to those first disciples in Jerusalem; however, we must realize there is a timeless promise to all who read those words. We have seen, we have heard, we have experienced, and now we must live our lives committed to the mission. We are not only recipients of the resurrection message, we are invited to be active participants in the resurrection mission. Luke's record of the first disciples' response can be found in Acts, a story of the active mission of the early disciples. The record of our response is still being written. How will you respond?

The story of Easter can transform our lives in the ways we have seen above. As we encounter the risen Christ, my prayer is that we allow Him to change us. I am thankful for the privilege of joining you in the journey. As we conclude our study, may we continue to write the story of the change that the risen Christ is making in our lives. There is a coming day that will change the title of this final chapter. The greatest day in history will be the day that Jesus returns, receiving us into His presence. Until that day, may we be powerful witnesses of Jesus Christ wherever we are and wherever He leads as we walk with Him.

LEARNING ACTIVITY

Identify ways your life is different because of Christ's resurrection.

List ways in which your life reflects one who has been changed by the resurrected Christ.

Questions for the Journey Ahead
1. Which of the encounters above (pp. 85-91) can you most relate to and why?

2. Which description best describes you—passive observer or powerful witness?

3. What are some specific things that you can do to allow God to transform you into a powerful witness?

4. Considering the face and the impact of the resurrection, what is Christ calling you to do for Him and His kingdom?

5. Who do needs to hear the reason for the hope that you have? Set times that you can pray for and talk with that person.

6. How is God calling you to change your life to demonstrate your commitment to the risen and returning Lord?

1. Quoted in Warren Wiersbe, *The Bible Exposition Commentary*, vol. 1 (Wheaton, IL: Victor Books 1989), 227.
2. Quoted at *www.sermoncentral.com*. Accessed January 25, 2012.

Jerusalem in the Time of Jesus

1. The Temple
2. Court of Women
3. Court of Gentiles
4. Eastern Gate
5. Garden of Gethsemane
6. Mount of Olives
7. Kidron Valley
8. Herod's Palace
9. Traditional Golgotha
10. Traditional Tomb of Jesus

ILLUSTRATOR ART/ BILL LATTA

Two Ways to Earn Credit
for Studying LifeWay Christian Resources Material

Christian Growth Study Plan resources are available for course credit for personal growth and church leadership training.

Courses are designed as plans for personal spiritual growth and for training current and future church leaders. To receive credit, complete the book, material, or activity. Respond to the learning activities or attend group sessions, when applicable, and show your work to your pastor, staff member, or church leader. Then go to *www.lifeway.com/CGSP*, or call the toll-free number for instructions for receiving credit and your certificate of completion.

For information about studies in the Christian Growth Study Plan, refer to the current catalog online at the CGSP Web address. This program and certificate are free LifeWay services to you.

CONTACT INFORMATION:
Christian Growth Study Plan
One LifeWay Plaza, MSN 117
Nashville, TN 37234
CGSP info line 1-800-968-5519
www.lifeway.com/CGSP
To order resources 1-800-485-2772

Need a CEU?

Receive Continuing Education Units (CEUs) when you complete group Bible studies by your favorite LifeWay authors.

Some studies are approved by the Association of Christian Schools International (ACSI) for CEU credits. Do you need to renew your Christian school teaching certificate? Gather a group of teachers or neighbors and complete one of the approved studies. Then go to *www.lifeway.com/CEU* to submit a request form or to find a list of ACSI-approved LifeWay studies and conferences. Book studies must be completed in a group setting. Online courses approved for ACSI credit are also noted on the course list. The administrative cost of each CEU certificate is only $10 per course.

CONTACT INFORMATION:
CEU Coordinator
One LifeWay Plaza, MSN 150
Nashville, TN 37234
Info line 1-800-968-5519
www.lifeway.com/CEU